D0948109

FLESH AND SPIRIT

FLESH AND SPIRIT

An Examination of Galatians 5.19-23

WILLIAM BARCLAY

The works of the flesh are these . . .
But the fruit of the Spirit is . . .

ABINGDON PRESS
Nashville   Tennessee

227.4
B244

FIRST PUBLISHED 1962
© SCM PRESS LTD 1962
PRINTED IN GREAT BRITAIN

CONTENTS

To My Friends
H. E. S. and H. G. S.
who daily obey the apostolic command
to practise hospitality
and who welcomed me
when I was a stranger

PREFACE

THIS book really consists of two separate halves. In November of 1959, at the invitation of the Divinity Faculty of the University College of North Wales, I had the privilege of delivering a series of lectures to the students at Bangor. I should be sadly lacking in courtesy and in gratitude if I did not express my very sincere thanks for that invitation, and for the most gracious and considerate hospitality which I received during the week I spent in Bangor. The welcome of staff and students alike I will not soon forget. The subject on which I chose to lecture was the words in the list of the fruit of the Spirit in Gal. 5.22, 23. The Rev. David L. Edwards, Editor of the SCM Press, suggested to me that these lectures might become a volume in the Religious Book Club, and he also suggested that I should add to them a similar study of the words in the list of the works of the flesh in the preceding verses of that chapter of Galatians. The fact that one half of this book was written expressly to be delivered as a series of lectures and that the other half was expressly written for publication as part of a book will explain any difference there is in the treatment of the material in the two halves.

I have dealt with certain of these words in previous books which I have written on words, but the treatment here is new and very much fuller.

My method has been to study these words in detail in the Septuagint, the Greek Old Testament, and in the great ethical Greek writers like Plato and Aristotle; to seek to illustrate them from the life and times of the ancient world contemporary with the writings of Paul; and to trace their usage in the New Testament itself.

This book is far from being a handbook of Christian Ethics, but I am convinced that any consideration and exposition of Christian Ethics must necessarily begin from as clear as possible a definition of the ethical terms of the New Testament.

It is therefore my hope that this book may do a very little to define the ethical terms on which the Christian ethic is founded, to show the background from which they arose, and to confront people with their challenge and their demand today.

I should like to place on record once again my continuing gratitude to the Rev. David L. Edwards and his staff for the continual help and encouragement which they have given me.

WILLIAM BARCLAY

Trinity College,
Glasgow
September 1961

ABBREVIATIONS

I HAVE consistently examined the translations of the words discussed in the modern translations of the Bible; and in referring to these translations I have used the following abbreviations:

NT: New Testament
OT: Old Testament
LXX: The Septuagint, the Greek Old Testament
AV: The Authorized Version
RV: The Revised Version
RSV: The Revised Standard Version
NEB: The New English Bible
M: The Moffatt translation
W: The translation by R. F. Weymouth
CKW: *The New Testament in Plain English* by Charles Kingsley Williams
P: *Letters to Young Churches* by J. B. Phillips

When translations of passages from the OT are different from the AV or from any of the modern versions, the reason is that such translations are regularly taken from the LXX, since it is the Greek usage of the words which is under consideration.

I

THE WAR IN THE SOUL

PHILOSOPHY and theology are essentially a transcript and an interpretation of human experience, and human experience is that there is a warfare in the human soul. To Paul that was a warfare between two opposing forces which he called the flesh and the spirit. 'The desires of the flesh are against the spirit,' he said, 'and the desires of the spirit are against the flesh, for these are opposed to each other' (Gal. 5.17). 'I delight in the law of God in my inmost self,' he says, 'but I see in my members another law at war with the law of my mind' (Rom. 7.22). Here to Paul was the dilemma of the human situation.

Paul was by no means the first person to see life in terms of internal conflict. The Jews had their doctrine of the *yetser hatobh* and the *yetser hara*, the good nature and the evil nature. In man, as they saw it, there were two natures, so that man was always in the situation of one who was being drawn in two directions at one and the same time. Man is in the most literal sense *distracted*, drawn apart. It is as if there stood beside him two angels, one a good angel beckoning him upwards, the other an evil angel seducing him downwards. So basic to humanity is this evil nature or impulse that the Rabbis believed that God himself had created it. The imagination of a man's heart is evil from his youth (Gen. 8.21). Rabbi Abahu interpreted the regret of God in Gen. 6.6 to mean that God actually regretted that he 'had put the bad leaven in the dough'. The evil impulse was waiting on a man as he emerged from the womb, for 'sin croucheth at the door', that is, the door of the womb (Gen. 4.7; *Sanhedrin* 91 b), and all through man's life it remained 'his implacable enemy' (Tanhuma, *Beshallah* 3). The warfare in the soul was part of the heritage of Jewish belief.

What was true of Hebrew thought was equally true of Greek thought. In the myth in the *Phaedrus* (246 B) Plato describes the soul as the charioteer whose task it is to drive in double harness two horses, one of whom is 'noble and of noble breed', and the other of whom is 'the opposite in breed and character'. The noble horse is reason, and the untamed horse is passion, and the horse of evil nature 'weighs the chariot down', and pulls it to the earth. Here again is the same picture of warfare and tension, always with the terrible possibility of ruin as its consequence.

This inner conflict runs like a kind of chorus through the writings both of the Romans and the Greeks. Ovid (*Metamorphoses* 7.20) uttered his famous sigh of frustration:

> *Video meliora, proboque;*
> *Deteriora sequor.*

'I see the better things, and I agree with them, but I follow the worse.' 'Men,' said Seneca, 'love and hate their vices at the same time' (*Letters* 112.3). According to Epictetus the beginning of philosophy stems from man's discovery of 'his impotence and weakness in necessary things' (*Discourses* 2.11.1).

What then is the reason for this warfare? Wherein lies the power of the evil force? To this question the ancient world unanimously answered that the evil and destructive power resides in the body of man. Here again is a transcript of human experience. Men knew only too well the number of temptations which attack a man through his body; men knew how much easier it would be to be 'good' if they were spiritualized creatures without a body.

The thought is there in later Judaism. 'A perishable body weighs down the soul, and this earthly tent burdens the thoughtful mind' (Wisd. 9.15).

The evil of the body became one of the dominant ideas of Greek thought. *Sōma sēma*, the body is a tomb, ran the Orphic jingle. The body, said Philolaus, is a house of detention in which the soul is imprisoned to expiate its sin. Epictetus can say that he is ashamed to have a body, that he is a 'poor soul shackled to a corpse' (*Fragment* 23). Seneca speaks of 'the detestable habitation' of the body, and vain flesh in which the soul is imprisoned (*Letters* 92.110). 'Disdain the flesh,' says Marcus Aurelius, 'blood and bones and network, a twisted skein of nerves, veins, arteries' (*Meditations* 2.2).

This attitude to the body is particularly embedded in two of the greatest of Greek writers and it so happens that they were writers who had an incalculable influence on Christian thought. It is there in Plato and in particular in the *Phaedo*. The *Phaedo* tells of the last hours of the life of Socrates, and in its earliest sections it is a statement of the desirability of death. It is only by death which rids men of the body that the philosopher can enter into knowledge and reality and truth. The study of philosophy is nothing other than the study of dying (*Phaedo* 64 A). The philosopher more than any other man seeks to separate the soul from communion with the body (64 E). It is only when the soul leaves the body, and avoids all possible association and contact with the body, when it strives to be alone by itself, that it can reach out to reality, for so long as it is with the body it is constantly deceived by the body (65 B, C, D). The companionship of the body disturbs the soul and hinders it from attaining truth and wisdom. The soul is contaminated by the body. If we are ever to know anything we must be freed from the body. The body is the fetter of the soul. The philosopher is in every way hostile to the body, and aims always to escape from this companionship which he hates (67 A, C, E; 68 A). No man can be a lover of wisdom and a lover of the body (68 C). Since all this is so, clearly a man must die to live. Platonic thought regarded the body as the supreme hindrance to wisdom and to truth.

The second of the great writers in whom this line of thought appears is Philo who was a near contemporary of Paul, and who is the deliberate bridge between Jewish and Greek thought. In his commentary on *The Wisdom of Solomon* (9.15) J. A. F. Gregg assembles certain typical passages from Philo in which this attitude appears. Philo writes: 'the chief cause of ignorance is the flesh and association with the flesh. Nothing presents such a hindrance to the growth of the soul as the flesh, for it is a kind of foundation of ignorance and stupidity on which all the evils are built. . . . Souls that bear the burden of the flesh are weighed down and oppressed till they cannot look up to the heavens, and have their heads forcibly dragged downwards, being rooted to the earth like cattle' (*De Gigantibus* 7). 'It is not easy to believe in God because of the mortal companion (that is, the flesh) with which we are yoked' (*Q.R.D.H.* 18). The body is a prison and a corpse (*De Migratione* 2; *De Agricultura* 5). Here is the same attitude again stated even more vividly and acutely.

Even in a poet like Virgil this same thought appears. There is a divine life principle which nourishes all living things, but it can be 'clogged by noxious bodies, blunted by earth-born limbs and dying members . . . shut up in the darkness and in a gloomy prison house' (*Aeneid* 6.730-734).

The ancient world was filled with a kind of horror and loathing of the body.

Let us now turn to Paul. In the OT and in the simpler thought of the Gospels man is composed of two parts. He is composed of the outward and visible part which is his body, and of an inner and unseen part which is his soul. The body will ultimately perish, but the soul lives on. Paul's division of man is more complicated. For him man is body, soul and spirit, *sōma*, *psuchē* and *pneuma* (1 Thess. 5.23).

The body is the outward and the material part of a man, and to its place in the thought of Paul we will presently return. The soul, the *psuchē*, is the principle of physical life. Properly speaking, every living creature has a *psuchē*. An animal has a *psuchē*; it might even be said that plants and growing things have *psuchē*; everything that lives has *psuchē*. *Psuchē* is that which joins a man to the animal creation of which in one part of his being he forms a part. For that reason Paul can use the word *psuchē* in two popular ways, which have a very close affinity with English colloquial usage.

(a) He can use it in the sense of *a living person*, much in the way in which we might say in English: 'I never saw a living soul', or as we might call an unfortunate person 'a poor soul'. The modern versions of the NT rightly obscure this, although the AV preserves it. Tribulation and anguish will come on *every soul of man* that doeth evil (Rom. 2.9). Here the RSV and the NEB have *every human being*. So the AV has: 'Let every *soul* be subject to the higher powers' (Rom. 13.1), in which passage the RSV and the NEB have simply *person*. In this usage *psuchē* simply means a living person, as we might say, for instance, that a ship foundered with three hundred souls.

(b) He sometimes uses *psuchē* simply in the sense of *life*, a usage which even the AV obscures. He says of Priscilla and Aquila that they risked their necks for his *life*, where the word for *life* is *psuchē* (Rom. 16.4). He says of Epaphroditus that he risked his *life* to complete the service of the Philippians to him, where again the word is *psuchē* (Phil. 2.30). The basic connection in Paul's thought of *psuchē* and physical life is quite clear.

Paul's use of the related adjective *psuchikos* underlines this. He speaks of the man who is *psuchikos* as being unable to receive the gifts of the Spirit of God (1 Cor. 2.14). There the AV translates the *natural* man; and the RSV and the NEB translate the *unspiritual* man. The man who is *psuchikos* is the man who is living on the purely natural level; his standards are the self-preservation and the self-centredness and the acquisitiveness which are characteristic of the animal.

To discover what Paul means by the spirit, the *pneuma*, is not altogether easy. The difficulty becomes clear when we consult different English or Greek texts of the NT, for the texts do not agree as to when spirit and *pneuma* are to be spelled with an initial capital letter, that is, as to when the reference is to the Spirit of God and to the spirit of man. This much is certain. The spirit is the ruling part of man; it is the spirit which controls the thoughts and the emotions, the mental activities and the passions of a man. Further, it is precisely the possession of this spirit which makes a man different from the animal creation; he shares *psuchē*, the life principle with the animals; but he alone possesses *pneuma*, for it is that which makes him man. Still further, the *pneuma* is the link between God and man; it is through the *pneuma* that God can speak to men and that men can have fellowship and communion with God.

The *pneuma* is the part of man which is distinctively and uniquely kin to God.

But the real problem is to know whether the *pneuma*, the spirit, is part of man as such, or whether it is only part of a man after he has become a Christian, whether the *pneuma* is part of human nature or whether it is the gift of God to redeemed human nature. J. E. Frame in his commentary on *I Thessalonians* (5.23) cites a passage from Theodore of Mopseuestia: 'God has never placed the three, soul, spirit and body in an unbeliever, but only in believers. Of these the soul and the body are natural, but the spirit is a special benefit (*euergesia*) to us, a gift of grace to those who believe.'

It is quite true that Paul repeatedly speaks of God sending his Spirit, or the Spirit of his Son, into our hearts. It is because God has sent the Spirit of his Son into our hearts that we can call him Father in the fullest and the most intimate sense of the term (Gal. 4.6). It is the Spirit dwelling in us who gives life to our mortal bodies (Rom. 8.11). Our bodies have become temples of the Holy Spirit (I Cor. 6.19). God has given us the earnest of the Spirit in our hearts (II Cor. 1.22). If this be the case, then a Christian is distinctively a man into whom this presence and this power have entered as it cannot enter into other men. It would then be true to say that the spirit of the Christian is nothing else than the Holy Spirit taking up his residence in the man, and giving his life a peace and a beauty and a power which are simply not available or possible for the non-Christian man.

There are two facts which make it very likely that that is indeed the thought that was in the mind of Paul.

(a) Paul has a curious way of speaking to his friends of 'your spirit', especially in his closing blessings. 'The grace of the Lord Jesus Christ be with your spirit' (Gal. 6.18; Phil. 4.23; Philemon 25). The spirit there is what we might call the Christian personality of Paul's friends. He writes to them and he blesses them not simply as men with *psuchē*, with physical life, but as men with *pneuma*, with spirit, men who, if we may put it so, are not only alive, but 'Christianly' alive.

(b) Paul has two words which he consistently uses in connection with the Spirit.

The first is the word *arrabōn* (II Cor. 1.22; 5.5; Eph. 1.14). The word *arrabōn* is a word from the world of business and of trade and of commerce. In any business transaction involving sale and purchase, or in any legal engagement involving the giving of services for an arranged sum, an *arrabōn* was paid. The *arrabōn* was the advance payment of a part of the price or a part of the fee in guarantee that in due time the full debt would be discharged. In point of fact the RSV translates *arrabōn* by the word *guarantee*, and the NEB by the word *pledge*. The gift of the Holy Spirit is therefore a foretaste of the fulness of life which the Christian will one day live in the presence of God, a foretaste of the very life of God himself, and a pledge and a guarantee that some day God will fulfil his promise and enable the Christian to enter into that life. He who is in the Spirit has, therefore, in him the very life of God.

The second is the word *sphragizein* which means *to seal*. Paul repeatedly speaks of the Christian as being sealed by the Holy Spirit, or with the Holy Spirit (II Cor. 1.22; Eph. 1.13; 4.30). In the ancient world of trade a seal was commonly used much as a trade-mark is used today. It was the sign of ownership, or the proof that an article was the product of a certain man or firm. So, for instance, jars of wine were sealed with the seal of the owner of the vineyard from which they came. This, then, means that the possession of the Holy Spirit is the guarantee that a man belongs to God. The possession of the Spirit is God's trade-mark upon a man. If a man has the Spirit, that man's life is the product of the workmanship of God.

In the thought of Paul the spirit of a man is that part of a man which is implanted in him by God; it is the presence and the power of God in him; it is the coming of the risen Christ into residence within the man. And the result of that is a link between the man and God which gives him a new fellowship with God and a new power to express that fellowship in strength and beauty of life.

This is set out most clearly in Paul's richest passage about the Holy Spirit and the spirit of man in Rom. 8.1-17. That passage gives us the perfect summary of the relationship between the Spirit of God and the spirit of man. Without the Spirit of Christ a man cannot begin to be a Christian at all (verse 9). It is the Spirit who makes him a son of God (verse 14), and who assures him of the reality of that sonship (verse 16). For the Christian man the Spirit must be the law of his life, his director, the standard by which he judges all things, the person whose gifts he most of all desires (verses 4, 5, 9). The Spirit brings him certain great gifts. The Spirit brings him *liberation* from the law of sin and death (verse 2). The man into whose life the Spirit has come is the man set free. The Spirit brings him *peace* (verse 6). The Spirit brings him victory in the warfare of the soul. The Spirit brings him *life*. His mortal body becomes alive with the life of Christ (verse 11). The non-Christian man without Christ and the Holy Spirit may be said to exist; he cannot be said to live. The Spirit brings him *power* (verse 13) and enables him to put to death the deeds of the body. The peace which the Spirit brings is the peace of conquest.

It may be said that for Paul the spirit of a man is the indwelling power of God in that man, or, to put it in another way, it is the risen Christ resident within him. The spirit of a man is that part of a man which has kinship with God, and which therefore gives a man fellowship with God and power to win the victory in the warfare of the soul.

THE ENEMY IN THE SOUL

WE have seen what Paul means by the *psuchē*, the soul, and by the *pneuma*, the spirit; we now turn to the third part of man, the *sōma*, the body. There are three ways in which Paul speaks of the body.

i. He speaks of it in a way which is perfectly neutral, and in which he simply means the physical body which

every man possesses. He speaks about the heathen dishon-
ouring their bodies with their sexual excesses and perversions (Rom. 1.24); he talks of the marks of persecution
which he bears in his own body (Gal. 6.17); he tells of Abraham knowing that the physical force of his body was as
good as dead (Rom. 4.19). Twice he uses the physical body
and its parts as symbolic of the Church as the Body of
Christ (Rom. 12.4, 5; I Cor. 12.12-27). In these passages the
body is simply the body in the physical sense of the term,
and no verdict is implied one way or the other.

ii. He speaks of the body in a way which implies the
imperfection and the danger of the body. He speaks of the
sinful body (Rom. 6.6); the mortal body (Rom. 6.12; 8.11);
the body doomed to death (Rom. 7.24); the body dead because of sin (Rom. 8.10). He declares that the body must
be subjected (I Cor. 9.27), and that the deeds of the body
must be put to death (Rom. 8.13). Here the body is viewed
as that part of a man which is in any event doomed to
death and decay, and there is the implication that the body
is greatly responsible for the sin of man and that there are
things connected with the body which must be eliminated
for ever in the Christian life.

iii. But in spite of this Paul never implies that the body
as such is incurable and fit for nothing but destruction. The
body can be redeemed (Rom. 8.23) and transformed (Phil.
3.21). The body can be taken and offered as a sacrifice to
God (Rom. 12.1), and with it and in it a man can glorify
God (I Cor. 6.20; Phil. 1.20). The body can be, and for the
Christian is, the temple of the Holy Spirit (I Cor. 6.19). It
is quite clear that for Paul the body is not essentially evil.
In its nature it will die. But it has tremendous potentialities
for good and for evil, according as it is dominated by sin
or dedicated to God. For Paul the body is itself quite neutral.
The direction in which it will go depends on which force
controls it for good or for evil.

But now we come to the much more difficult word, *sarx*,
the flesh. Here is one of the characteristic words of Paul,
one of the words which run through his letters, and especially through the letters to the Romans, the Galatians and
the Corinthians. It is a word of which there is no adequate

English translation, a word of which the meaning cannot be sharply and simply defined, a word towards the meaning of which we have to grope our way, and yet a word which stands for certain facts in the human situation which are part of the basic experience of life of every man. Let us then seek to penetrate into its meaning. We may begin with two fundamental facts about it.

i. *Sarx* is the deadly enemy of *pneuma*. The warfare in the soul is precisely between flesh, to use the ordinary translation of the word, and spirit. 'These,' says Paul, 'are opposed to each other' (Gal. 5.17). Whatever else is true, these two are the opposing forces in the being of man.

ii. *Sarx* is very much more than the body. In the thought of Paul the sins of the flesh include far more than the fleshly sins which have to do with the body. When Paul lists the works of the flesh he certainly begins with immorality, impurity and licentiousness, but he goes on from there to enmity, strife, jealousy, anger, the party spirit which are not sins of the body at all. The sins of the flesh in the normal modern sense of the term are far from being the only sins of the flesh in the Pauline sense of the term. It is in fact true to say that they are not even the main and the most serious sins of the flesh.

iii. Paul does use the term to denote a bodily or a physical condition. He speaks of circumcision in the flesh, as compared with circumcision in the heart (Rom. 2.28). He speaks of a thorn in the flesh, by which he means a bodily ailment (RSV) or illness (NEB) (Gal. 4.13). There are times when Paul uses *sarx* where he might just as well have used *sōma*, and where its meaning is physical without any real overtones or implications.

iv. Paul uses *sarx* in phrases which in English we might express by 'humanly speaking', or 'from the human point of view'. Thus Jesus was descended from David according to the flesh (Rom. 1.3). Abraham is our forefather according to the flesh (Rom. 4.1). Jesus is a Jew according to the flesh (Rom. 9.5). When *sarx* is used like that, it always implies that this is not the whole story, that there is something more to be said, that what is said is true from the human point of view although it is not the whole truth.

v. Paul uses *sarx* in phrases and contexts in which we would use some such phrase as 'to judge by human standards'. Not many wise men after the flesh are called into the Church (I Cor. 1.26), that is, not many who are wise according to worldly standards (RSV), or by any human standard (NEB). Paul in writing to the Corinthians defends himself against the possible charge of purposing according to the flesh (II Cor. 1.17), that is, making plans like a worldly man who is ready to alter and to change as expediency may suggest. He writes to the Corinthians that now he knows no man, not even Christ, after the flesh (II Cor. 5.16). This the RSV translates: 'We regard no one from a human point of view', and the NEB: 'Worldly standards have ceased to count in our estimate of any man.' In such phrases the flesh stands for the human standard, the human point of view, the human evaluation.

vi. Paul uses *sarx* where the main thought is that of humanity. The expression: 'By deeds of the law no flesh shall be justified in God's sight' (Rom. 3.20; Gal. 2.16; I Cor. 1.29) is a Hebraism and a normal Jewish turn of speech where modern speech would say 'no human being'. So Jesus came in the likeness of sinful flesh (Rom. 8.3), where the idea is that Christ took our humanity upon him. Hebrew would always prefer a concrete to an abstract expression, and, therefore, prefers to speak of flesh rather than of humanity.

vii. We now come to the unique and distinctive Pauline use of the word *sarx*, Paul's conception of *sarx* as the supreme enemy in the warfare in the soul. Let us then see how Paul uses the word in this special sense.

(a) It may be said that to live in the flesh is the precise opposite of being a Christian. 'You are not in the flesh; you are in the Spirit' (Rom. 8.9, 12). It is the non-Christian man who lives in the flesh. Paul can look back on the time 'while we were living in the flesh' (Rom. 7.5; 8.5). The Christian has crucified the flesh with its passions and desires (Gal. 5.24). To live in the flesh is the exact opposite of to live in the Spirit, in Christ, to be a Christian.

(b) To put it even more widely, to be in the flesh is to be under sin (Rom. 7.14). To be dominated by the flesh and to be the slave of sin are one and the same thing.

(c) The flesh is the great enemy of the good life, and of the Christian life. It is this *sarx* which renders the law impotent (Rom. 8.3). That is to say, it is this *sarx* which is responsible for that ever-repeated human situation in which a man quite clearly knows what to do and is yet quite helpless to do it. In the *sarx* nothing good dwells (Rom. 7.18). If we take this as a general statement, then it is exactly here that we see the difference between *sōma* and *sarx*, body and flesh. The body can become the instrument of the service and the glory of God; the flesh cannot. The body can be purified and even glorified; the flesh must be eliminated and eradicated. It is with the flesh that a man serves the law of sin (Rom. 7.25). It is the *sarx* which renders a man quite incapable of assimilating the teaching which he ought to be able to receive (I Cor. 3.1-3). The *sarx* cannot please God (Rom. 8.8). Worse than that, the *sarx* is essentially hostile to God (Rom. 8.7). Jealousy and strife and bitterness are the proof that a man or a community is living in the *sarx* (I Cor. 3.3).

It is quite clear that here we have a very considerable problem in translation. The AV, the RSV, Moffatt and Kingsley Williams on the whole retain the word flesh and the adjective fleshly. The *Twentieth Century New Testament*, Weymouth, Phillips, and the NEB ring the changes on such phrases as 'the lower nature', 'the earthly nature', 'the unspiritual nature', 'sinful nature', 'carnal attitude', 'the weakness of human nature'. There are undoubtedly a series of passages in particular in Galatians in which the idea of the lower nature serves very well. The RSV translates Gal. 5.13: 'Do not use your freedom as an opportunity for the flesh.' The NEB translates it: 'Do not turn your freedom into licence for your lower nature.' The RSV translates Gal. 5.16: 'Walk by the Spirit and do not gratify the desires of the flesh.' The NEB translates: 'If you are guided by the Spirit you will not fulfil the desires of your lower nature.' The RSV translates Gal. 5.24: 'Those who belong to Christ Jesus have crucified the flesh with its passions and desires.' The NEB translates: 'Those who belong to Christ Jesus have crucified the lower nature with its passions and desires.' The RSV translates Gal. 6.8: 'He who sows to his own flesh will from the flesh reap corruption; but he who sows to the Spirit will from the Spirit reap eternal life.' The NEB translates: 'If he sows in the field of his lower nature, he will reap from it a harvest of corruption, but if he sows in the field of the Spirit, the Spirit will bring him a harvest of eternal life.' In all these cases the translation of *sarx* by lower nature comes in aptly and relevantly.

What then is the flesh? Clearly the flesh is not the body. It is equally clear, if the thought of Paul is consistent, that the flesh is not the natural man, for Paul did say that the natural man, the unchristian man, the pagan man, need not necessarily be totally bad. Even in such a condition there are times when man can do by nature what the law requires, because the requirements of the law are written on his heart, and because even in such a condition man possesses conscience (Rom. 2.14, 15). To conceive of the flesh as the lower nature is not entirely satisfactory. To do so implies that there is in man a nature which is capable of goodness, just as there is a nature which is doomed to evil. The trouble about such a view is that the rot, in spite of all that we have said about the natural man, is all through human nature; the entire structure is tainted. It is entirely significant that Paul speaks of the *works* of the flesh and the *fruit* of the Spirit (Gal. 5.19, 22). A *work* is something which a man produces for himself; a fruit is something which is produced by a power which he does not possess. Man cannot *make* a fruit. That is to say, man can easily enough produce evil for himself, he cannot help doing so; but goodness has to be produced for him by a power which is not his power. The truth is that, while the translation 'the lower nature' frequently makes good sense, it does not go far enough.

The essence of the flesh is this. No army can invade a country from the sea unless it can obtain a bridgehead. Temptation would be powerless to affect men, unless there was some thing already in man to respond to temptation. Sin could gain no foothold in a man's mind and heart and soul and life unless there was an enemy within the gates who was willing to open the door to sin. The flesh is exactly the bridgehead through which sin invades the human personality. The flesh is like the enemy within the gates who opens the way to the enemy who is pressing in through the gates.

But where does this bridgehead come from? Where does this enemy within spring from? It is the universal experience of life that a man by his conduct fits or unfits himself to receive any experience. He makes himself such that he will or will not respond to certain experiences. The flesh is what man has made himself in contrast with man as God made him. The flesh is man as he has allowed himself to become in contrast with man as God meant him to be. The flesh stands for the total effect upon man of his own sin and of the sin of his fathers and of the sin of all men who have gone before him. The flesh is human nature as it has become through sin. Man's sin, his own sin and the sin of mankind, has, as it were, made him vulnerable to sin. It has made him fall even when he knew he was falling and even when he did not want to fall. It has made him such that he can neither avoid the fascination of sin nor resist the power of sin. The flesh stands for human nature weakened, vitiated, tainted by sin. The flesh is man as he is apart from Jesus Christ and his Spirit.

II

THE WORKS OF THE FLESH

B E F O R E we begin to examine the list of the works of the flesh as they are listed in Gal. 5.19-21 in individual detail there are two preliminary facts which we may note.

First, the list in the AV contains two sins which are not included in any of the lists in the modern translations from the RV onwards. At the beginning the AV has *moicheia*, adultery, and after envy it has murders, *phonoi*. These should not be included in the list as they appear in only few and late manuscripts.

Second, in examining the differences between the different translations it will be seen that sometimes some of the words appear in the singular and sometimes in the plural. This is not due to different manuscript readings, nor is it due to error or inaccuracy in translation. It is due to a habit of the Greek language. When a Greek abstract noun is used in the plural it often means manifestations or demonstrations or examples of that quality which the singular noun denotes. For instance, *thumos*, which is the singular form, means temper, and *thumoi*, which is the plural form, means outbursts of temper. *Phthonos* means envy, and *phthonoi* means displays of envy. Many of the words in the list of the works of the flesh are actually plural forms, and mean displays and acts of the quality which they denote. It is therefore possible to translate them in English either by the singular or the plural form, and sometimes in point of fact the singular is the more correct English idiom.

We now proceed to examine them one by one.

*   *   *

PORNEIA

AV, RV, NEB, W, CKW: fornication; RSV: immorality; M: sexual vice; P: sexual immorality.

Porneia is here used as a quite general word for unlawful and immoral sexual intercourse and relationships. The probable derivation of the word sheds a significant flood of light on the attitude of mind behind it. *Porneia* is prostitution, and *porne* is a prostitute. The likelihood is that these words are all connected with the verb *pernumi* which means to sell. Essentially *porneia* is the love which is bought and sold—which is not love at all. The great and basic error of this is that the person with whom such love is gratified is not really considered as a person at all, but as a thing. He or she is a mere instrument through which the demands of lust and passion are satisfied. True love is the total union of two personalities so that they become one person, and so that each finds its own fulfilment in union with the other. *Porneia* describes the relationship in which one of the parties can be purchased as a thing is purchased and discarded as a thing is discarded and where there is neither union of, nor respect for, personality.

It is significant that it is with this sin that Paul begins. The sexual life of the Graeco-Roman world in NT times was a lawless chaos. J. J. Chapman, describing the time in which Lucian lived, in the first half of the second century, writes: 'Lucian lived in an age when shame seems to have vanished from the earth.'

In Greece there had never been any shame in relationships before marriage or outside marriage. Demosthenes writes as if it was the merest commonplace, as indeed it was: 'We keep mistresses for pleasure, concubines for the day-to-day needs of the body, but we have wives in order to produce children legitimately and to have a trustworthy guardian of our homes' (*Against Neaera*, quoted, Athenaeus, *Deipnosophistae* 573 B). In the early days of Rome things had been very different and purity had been the rule. But in this the conquered had conquered the conquerors, and Rome learned to sin from Greece. 'I see Rome,' said Livy the historian, 'proud Rome, perishing the victim of her own prosperity' (3.13). It is hardly possible to mention a great Greek figure who had not his *hetaira*, his mistress, and often these mistresses were the most beautiful and the most cultured women of their day. Alexander the Great had his Thais, who after his death married Ptolemy of Egypt and became the mother of kings; Aristotle had his Herpyllia, Plato his Archeaenassa, Pericles his Aspasia, who, it was said, even wrote his speeches for him, Sophocles his Archippe whom he left his heiress, Isocrates his Metaneira. Phryne, the most famous of courtesans was so wealthy that she offered to build a wall round Thebes, if the Thebans would inscribe upon it: 'Whereas Alexander destroyed it, Phryne the courtesan restored it' (Athenaeus, *Deipnosophistae* 576-592). The Greek attitude can hardly be better shown than by the fact that, when Solon was the first to legalize prostitution and to open state brothels, the profits from them were used to erect temples to the gods (Athenaeus, *Deipnosophistae* 569 D).

When Greek laxity invaded Rome, it was sadly coarsened. Hiberina, says Juvenal, will no more be satisfied with one man than she would be with one eye (Juvenal, *Satires* 6.55). Roman women, says Seneca, were married to be divorced and were divorced to be married. Some of them distinguished the years, not by the names of the consuls, but by the names of their husbands. 'Chastity is simply a proof of ugliness' (Seneca, *On Benefits* 3.16.1-3). Innocence, says Seneca, is not rare, it is non-existent (*On Anger* 2.8). Juvenal paints the picture of the Roman woman passing the altar of Modesty with a cynical smile (Juvenal, *Satires* 6.308). 'The greater the infamy, the wilder the delight,' said Tacitus (Tacitus, *Annals* 11.26). The day was to come when Clement of Alexandria was to speak of certain women as the personification of adultery, 'girt like Venus with a golden girdle of vice' (Clement of Alexandria, *Paedagogus* 3.2.4). The day was to come when Alexander Severus, one of the great and good Emperors, was to supply a man when he entered upon a provincial governorship with 'twenty pounds of silver, six she-mules, a pair of mules, a pair of horses, two garments for use in the forum, two for use at home, one for the bath, one hundred gold pieces, one cook, one muleteer, and one concubine in the case of a man who had no wife and could not live without a woman' (*Scriptores Historiae Augustae, Alexander Severus* 42). The upper stratum of Roman society had become largely promiscuous. Even Messalina the Empress, the wife of Claudius, slipped out of the royal palace at nights to serve in a public brothel. She was the last to leave, and would 'return to the imperial pillow with all the odours of the stews' (Juvenal, *Satires* 6.114-132).

Still worse was the unnatural vice which was rampant. It began in the imperial household. Caligula notoriously lived in habitual incest with his sister Drusilla, and the lust of Nero did not even spare his mother Agrippina (Suetonius, *Caligula* 34; *Nero* 28).

From the highest to the lowest society was riddled with homosexuality. This was a vice which Rome learned from Greece. J. J. Döllinger calls it 'the great national disease of Greece' (J. J. Döllinger, *The Gentile and the Jew*, II, p. 239). J. J. Chapman says that in Greece this degeneration was 'not personal but racial', 'until it had become indigenous and ingrown'. He likens it to a loathesome fungus spreading steadily through a forest (J. J. Chapman, *Lucian, Plato and Greek Morals*, pp. 132, 133). In one of his dialogues Lucian makes Lycinus relate : 'It were better not to need marriage, but to follow Plato and Socrates and to be content with the love of boys' (Lucian, *The Lapiths* 39). In another dialogue Lucian brings on the stage the figure representing Socrates. 'I am a lover of boys,' he says, 'and wise in matters of love.' 'What is your attitude to pretty boys?' he is asked. 'Their kisses,' he answers, 'shall be the guerdon for the bravest after they have done some splendid reckless deed' (Lucian, *Philosophies for Sale* 15, 17). Plato's *Symposium* ranks as one of the great works of literature. Its subject is love, but it is homosexual love. Phaedrus begins the subject. 'I know not,' he says, 'any greater blessing to a young man who is beginning life than a virtuous lover, or to the lover than a beloved boy' (Plato, *Symposium* 178 D).

Gibbon writes : 'Of the first fifteen Emperors, Claudius was the only one whose taste in love was entirely correct.'

Julius Caesar was notoriously the lover of King Nicomedes of Bithynia. 'The queen's rival', they called him and his passion was the subject of the ribald songs the soldiers sang. Nero 'married' a castrated youth called Sporus and went in marriage procession with him throughout the streets of Rome, and he himself was 'married' to a freedman called Doryphorus. He went so far as to 'imitate the lamentations of a maiden being deflowered, and in public to perform the most intimate acts of this unspeakable union' (Suetonius, *Nero* 28, 29). The historian speaks of Hadrian's 'passion for males and the adulteries with married women to which he was addicted'. Hadrian's passion for the youth Antinous was notorious, and, when Antinous was drowned, Hadrian actually had him deified and oracles were given in his name (*Scriptores Historiae Augustae, Hadrian* 11, 14). Alexander Severus considered passing legislation to prohibit all catamites, but in the end decided not to, for he believed that the vice would only be driven underground since the passions of men would make it impossible to eliminate it (*Scriptores Historiae Augustae, Alexander Severus* 24).

It is to be noted that all the evidence which we have adduced for the unspeakable sexual immorality of the world contemporary with the New Testament comes, not from Christian writers, but from pagans who were disgusted with themselves.

Against this sexual immorality Paul's face is set. He is appalled that the Corinthians are not appalled at the case in which a man is living with his father's wife (I Cor. 5.1). Of this sin a man must repent or his so-called Christian life is a mockery (II Cor. 12.21). The Christian must totally abstain from it (I Thess. 4.3); he must shun it (I Cor. 6.18); he must put its deeds to death (Col. 3.5). It is the one sin in which a man clearly and unmistakably sins against his own body (I Cor. 6.18), and the body is not for immorality, it is for the Lord (I Cor. 6.13).

It has been said that chastity was the one completely new virtue which Christianity introduced into the pagan world. And there were three reasons why the task of introducing it was of quite extraordinary difficulty.

(i) There was no strong body of opinion against immorality. To the Graeco-Roman world immorality in sexual matters was not immorality; it was established custom and practice.

(ii) The prevalence of Gnostic ideas was a serious problem. The Gnostic saw spirit as altogether good and matter as essentially bad. If matter is essentially bad, then the body is necessarily evil. If that is so, there are two possibilities. First, there is the possibility of rigid asceticism in which every desire of the body is rigidly and strenuously denied. Second, there is the possibility that a man may argue that, since the body is bad, it does not matter what he does with it. He can glut and sate its appetites and it is of no importance, for the body is in any event a perishing and an evil thing. It is therefore clear that in one direction Gnosticism could be a defence of immorality.

One thing is clear, no Gnostic could ever speak of the body being for the Lord (I Cor. 6.13). For the Gnostic the body was the one part of man which could never be for the Lord. The Christian message of the salvation of the total personality, of the whole man, of body, soul and spirit was a new thing, and it necessarily involved a gospel of purity.

(iii) Christianity had to face a situation in which in many cases prostitution was connected with religion. There were many temples which had their crowds of sacred prostitutes. The Temple of Aphrodite in Corinth had a thousand of them, and they came down to the city streets to ply their trade each evening. The custom springs from the glorification of God in the life force which is clearest of all in the power of sex. Christianity had to face a situation in which religion and sexual immorality went hand in hand.

No one need be surprised that Paul begins his list of the works of the flesh with the sexual sins. He lived in a world in which such sin was rampant, and in that world Christianity brought men an almost miraculous power to live in purity.

AKATHARSIA

AV, RV, CKW : uncleanness; RSV, NEB, M, W : impurity; P : impurity of mind. Other translations of other occurrences of the word—NEB : vileness (Rom. 1.24), unclean lives (II Cor. 12.21), foul desires (Eph. 4.19), base motives (I Thess. 2.3), indecency (Eph. 5.3; Col. 3.5); P : sexual immorality (Eph. 5.3), dirty-mindedness (Col. 3.5).

Akatharsia is a word which began in the physical world, made its way into the ritual and the ceremonial world, and finished up in the moral world.

i. *Akatharsia* begins by meaning physical and material dirt. In the papyri, for instance, in a contract concerning the transfer of ownership of a house, the outgoing tenant undertakes to leave the house clean from all *akatharsia*. The house is to be left clean and free from dirt. Closely connected with this is the medical use of the word. It is used of the impure material which gathers round a sore or a wound (Hippocrates, *Fract.* 31). Plato uses it of the impurities which gather in the body, for which the spleen acts as a kind of absorbent (Plato, *Timaeus* 72 C). *Akatharsia*, therefore, is dirt or dirtiness in the physical sense of the term.

ii. *Akatharsia* in the Greek OT denotes ritual and ceremonial impurity oftener than anything else. There are about twenty instances of it in Leviticus, and they all refer to such impurity. It is, for instance, used of the uncleanness of unclean beasts (Lev. 20.25). It is used of the state of a woman in a menstrual condition (Lev. 18.19). Here something significant emerges. It is true that here the reference is to the taboos which make a person or a creature or a thing ceremonially unclean. But the essential point about this ceremonial uncleanness is that, when a person is in such a condition, he or she cannot approach God. In such a condition the person cannot enter the Temple and cannot share in the worship of the people. To seek to do so is to incur the wrath of God (Lev. 22.3). In the ritual sense, then, *akatharsia* is that which makes it impossible for a person to come into the presence of God; it shuts him off from God.

iii. Finally *akatharsia* enters the moral world. It is used for the lewdness of a loose and immoral woman (Hos. 2.10); it is used of the moral uncleanness which destroys a nation (Micah 2.10). There is a good instance of it in the Proverbs, where it is said of the foolish man : 'He rejoices in all things which God hates, and he is ruined by reason of *impurity* of soul' (Prov. 6.16).

It is not common in the classical writers, but Demosthenes uses it of the intolerable vileness of a man who has blatantly perjured himself to injure a friend, and who hypocritically pretends still to be his friend (Demosthenes, *Against Meidias* 119). Here *akatharsia* stands for a moral depravity which disgusts the person who sees it.

In this word *akatharsia*, then, there are three ideas.

i. It is the quality of that which is soiled and dirty. There is a kind of mind which is itself soiled and which soils everything which passes through it. It can reduce the finest action to a mean motive, and it can defile the purest things with a smutty jest.

ii. In this impurity there is a certain repulsive quality. It awakens disgust and loathing in any decent person who looks at it. There is a type of person who sometimes thinks he is being clever when in point of fact he is merely inducing in the minds of those who listen to him and who have contact with him an inward shudder of disgust.

iii. In this word there remains the idea of that which separates a man from God. Before it entered the moral world, *akatharsia*, as we have seen, described the ritual and the ceremonial uncleanness which according to the taboos of the time debarred a man from the presence of God. In the moral world the same idea still attaches to the word. 'Blessed are the pure in heart, for they shall see God' (Matt. 5.8). The sinner who repents will never find God far away, but the sinner who glories in his impurity has erected a barrier between himself and God.

ASELGEIA

AV, RV: lasciviousness; RSV: licentiousness; NEB, W, CKW: indecency; M, P: sensuality.
Other translations—P: lustfulness (II Cor. 12.21).

In the three words with which the list of the works of the flesh opens, Lightfoot sees a climax of evil. *Porneia* indicates sin within a specific area of life, the area of sexual relationships; *akatharsia* indicates a general defilement of the whole personality, tainting every sphere of life; *aselgeia* indicates a love of sin so reckless and so audacious that a man has ceased to care what God or man thinks of his actions. A man, he says, may be *akathartos*, impure, unclean, and hide his sin, for public opinion and public decency still have some hold upon him; but a man does not become *aselgēs* (the adjective) until he shocks public decency. As Lightfoot sees it, the essence of *aselgeia* is that it has come to such a stage of sinning that it makes no attempt whatever to hide or cloak its sin; it is sin lost to shame. Let us then investigate the word.

It does not appear at all in the canonical books of the Greek OT. In the apocryphal books it occurs twice. In Wisd. 14.26 sex perversion, disorder in marriage, adultery and *debauchery* (*aselgeia*) are linked together and there the connection is with sexual sin. In III Macc. 2.26 it is used more generally for audacious acts of impiety.

In the NT it occurs in Rom. 13.13 where it is said that the Christian cannot live in revelling and drunkenness, debauchery and *licentiousness*, quarrelling and jealousy. There the words go in pairs and *aselgeia* is in the pair which have to do with sexual sin. In II Cor. 12.21 it occurs in the trio impurity, immorality and *licentiousness*, and there again the reference is to sexual excess. In Eph. 4.19 it has a wider reference, for there licentiousness is said to be greedy to practise every kind of uncleanness. In the NT it does seem to be linked with sexual excess.

When we turn to the word in the classical writers, its range is much wider. Plato uses it of the sheer *impudence* of lawlessness (*Republic* 424 E). Demosthenes uses it of the *brutality* of an evil man, and of the arrogant *insolence* of Philip of Macedon (*Against Meidias* 21; *First Philippic* 4). The Greeks themselves defined it as 'audacious and insulting violence'. Basil defines it as 'a disposition of the soul which neither possesses nor can endure the pain of discipline' (Basil, *Reg. Brev. Int.* 67). It is defined as meaning 'readiness to indulge in any pleasure'.

There are certain usages of the word which vividly give its flavour. Plutarch uses it of Alcibiades who in his wild wantonness was completely regardless of public decency and public opinion (Plutarch, *Alcibiades* 8). Josephus uses it twice in a most revealing way. He uses it of Jezebel (*Antiquities of the Jews* 8.13.1). He uses it of a notorious act of a Roman soldier in the Temple precincts. The soldier on guard during certain Temple festivities publicly relieved himself, thereby insulting ordinary public decency, and what was worse, shamelessly defiling the holy place (*Antiquities of the Jews* 20.5.3). It may be that the way in which Demosthenes uses the word *aselgōs*, the adverb, is most revealing of all. He speaks of a man who was living *aselgōs*, and says of him that he was the kind of man into whose company no sensible man would ever take his daughter (Demosthenes, *Against Boeotus* 2.57).

Here, then, is the meaning of *aselgeia*; it denotes sin so open and so blatant that it has ceased to have any regard for what anyone may think or feel or say. So then we may distinguish three characteristics of *aselgeia*.

i. It is wanton and undisciplined action. It is the action of a man who is at the mercy of his passions and his impulses and his emotions, and in whom the voice of calm reason has been silenced by the storms of self-will.

ii. It has respect neither for the persons nor the rights of anyone else. It is violent, insolent, abusive, audacious. Any thought and any sympathy for the feelings of others has ceased to exist.

iii. It is completely indifferent to public opinion and to public decency. A man may well begin to do a wrong thing in secret; at the beginning his one aim and desire may be to hide it from the eyes of men. He may love the wrong thing, and he may even be mastered by it, but he is still ashamed of it. But it is perfectly possible for him to come to a stage when he does openly and blatantly that which he did secretly and in concealment. He may come to a stage of sin when he is so lost to shame that he no longer cares what others see, and what they may say, or what they may think. The terrible thing about *aselgeia* is that it is the act of a character which has lost that which ought to be its greatest defence—its self-respect, and its sense of shame.

EIDŌLOLATREIA

AV, RV, RSV, NEB, M : idolatry; W : idol worship; CKW : worship of idols; P : worship of false gods.

On the face of it the worship of idols seems hard for a modern man to understand. It is difficult to understand how any man could regard with reverence a piece of wood or stone or metal, however beautiful the shape into which it was carved and however costly its adornment and ornamentation. It becomes even more difficult to understand when we remember that many ancient idols were anything but beautiful. For instance, the image of Artemis or Diana in the famous temple at Ephesus was a black, squat, uncouth figure, covered with many breasts, and totally unbeautiful.

The fact is that in the beginning no one worshipped *the idol*. An idol had two functions. It was meant to *localize* the god it represented, and it was meant to *visualize* the god it represented. Originally the idol was never meant to be worshipped. It was simply meant to make it easier for a man to worship the god whom it represented by giving him something visible localized in a definite place. But once that had been done, it was almost inevitable that a man should go on to worship the idol rather than the god whom it represented. Take, for example, the development of Emperor worship in the Roman Empire. This began as an expression of gratitude for the safety, the security, the justice and the good order Rome had brought to men. Rome cleared the seas of pirates and the roads of brigands. She

B

brought even-handed justice to replace the caprice of ty-
rants. So grateful were men to Rome for her strong arm and
her impartial justice that there were kings who willed their
countries to the Romans when they died. Out of this gratitude there came the worship of the goddess Roma, the spirit
of Rome; and this worship existed more than a century before actual Emperor worship arose. But men are eager for
something to see; and Rome and the spirit of Rome were,
as it were, incarnated in the Emperor. And so worship came
to be transferred to the Emperor himself, a phenomenon
which in the beginning embarrassed the Roman Emperors
and to which they tried to put an end. But to those on the
outskirts of the Empire the Emperor was no more than a
name; and so his statue was erected, and worship was transferred to the statue. First the unseen spirit of Rome, then
the visible Emperor, then the present statue—that was the
course of development.

And here is the first basic error of idol worship—idol
worship is the worship of the created thing rather than of
the Creator of all things. This is precisely what Paul saw in
his sketch of the genesis of idol worship:

> What can be known about God is plain to them, because
> God has shown it to them. Ever since the creation of the
> world his invisible nature, namely, his eternal power and
> deity, has been clearly perceived in the things that have
> been made. So they are without excuse; for although
> they knew God they did not honour him as God or give
> thanks to him, but they became futile in their thinking
> and their senseless minds were darkened. Claiming to be
> wise, they became fools, and exchanged the glory of the
> immortal God for images resembling mortal man or birds
> or animals or reptiles (Rom. 1.19-23).

This kind of idolatry still exists, for basically this kind of
idolatry is the worship of things instead of the worship of
God. A man's God may rightly be said to be that to which
he dedicates his time, his substance and his talents, that to
which he gives himself. Into our language there has come
in recent times a new phrase, a status symbol. A status sym-

bol is something which a man desires as the outward proof and guarantee that he has reached a certain stage of success. The status symbol may be a house in a certain district of a town, a car of a certain make, some kind of piece of furniture or household goods which is coveted by many but achieved by few. It may well be said that this status symbol is the man's idol, for it is to the gaining of it that he dedicates himself. Whenever any *thing* in the world begins to hold the principal place in our hearts and minds and aims, then that thing has become an idol, for that thing has usurped the place which belongs to God.

It is interesting and it is significant that idol worship comes immediately after the group of words which describe the sexual sins. In the ancient world idol worship and sexual immorality were closely connected. The writer of the Wisdom of Solomon says: 'The idea of making idols was the beginning of fornication, and the invention of them was the corruption of life' (Wisd. 14.12). Whence comes this connection?

We can see this connection in the OT. It emerges vividly, pictorially and dramatically in the poetry of the second chapter of Hosea. The mother, that is, Israel, has said: 'I will go after my lovers, who give me my bread and my water, my wool and my flax, my oil and my wine.' Then the voice of God goes on: 'She did not know that it was I who gave her the grain, the wine and the oil' (Hos. 2.5, 8). In Palestine in the ancient pre-Israelite worship, the Baals were fertility gods. They were the gods of the forces behind the growing of the harvest. It was they who gave the corn, the wine and the oil. To them Israel turned, and since Israel was the bride of God, she could be said to go a-whoring after strange gods, and therefore adultery became the symbol for apostasy, for apostasy was infidelity in which Israel turned from the God who was her true husband to seek a husband among the false gods.

Now, as we have already noticed, of all the powers of growth that of sex is the most vivid, and vital, and powerful. To that end the sexual act became an act of worship and of glorification of God; and therefore the stocking of the ancient shrines with sacred prostitutes became the custom and sexual intercourse with them became a kind of act of worship of the power of the force of life.

The attraction of a worship like this to the lower part of human nature is quite obvious. Natural man would much prefer this to the bleak austerities of true worship. Herein lay the terrible danger of Baal worship against which the prophets pleaded and thundered.

The tragedy of idol worship was twofold. In it men worshipped the created thing instead of the Creator of all things, and in it men used as worship an act in itself lovely in such a way that it became a sin. At one stroke idol worship destroyed true worship and destroyed that purity which is the highest worship of all.

PHARMAKEIA

AV, P: witchcraft; RV, RSV, NEB, W: sorcery; M, CKW: magic. The word *pharmakeia* followed a process of degeneration in meaning. *Pharmakon* is a drug, and *pharmakeia* is the use of drugs. There are three stages in the meaning of the word.

i. *Pharmakeia* is used medically with no bad meaning at all. Plato talks of the different kinds of medical treatment, cautery, incision, *the use of drugs*, starvation (Plato, *Protagoras* 354 A). He gives it as his opinion that non-dangerous diseases should never be further complicated by the use of drugs (Plato, *Timaeus* 89 B). At this stage *pharmakeia* is simply a medical word for the medical use of drugs.

ii. The word then begins to denote the misuse of drugs, that is, the use of drugs to poison and not to cure. So we read about the law regarding poisoning (Plato, *Laws* 933 B), and Demosthenes accuses a bad man of poisoning and all kinds of villainy (Demosthenes 40.57). This is the beginning of the bad use of the word.

iii. Finally, the word takes the meaning of sorcery and witchcraft. It is, for instance, repeatedly used of the Egyptian sorcerers and charmers who competed with Moses when Pharaoh would not let Israel go (Ex. 7.11, 22; 8.18; Wisd. 7.12; 18.13); and this magic and witchcraft and sorcery is one of the sins for which Isaiah foretells the destruction of Babylon by the wrath of God (Isa. 47.9, 12). The word has gone full circle. From meaning a healing and a curative drug it has come to mean a vicious and malignant dealing in witchcraft and sorcery.

Christianity grew up in an age in which the use of sorcery and the magical arts was widespread, and often criminal in its intent. We hear little or nothing about sorcery and witchcraft and magic in the early centuries of Greek literature. Pliny has a story that magic was introduced into Greece by a certain Persian named Osthanes in the time of the Persian Wars (Pliny, *Natural History* 30.1). The first reference to criminal sorcery is in the speeches of Demosthenes. In the speech against Aristogeiton he refers to Theoris of Lemnos, 'the filthy sorceress', who was duly put to death because of her evil ways.

In Rome as far back as the Twelve Tables we find a regulation forbidding the charming away of another person's crops (Seneca, *Natural Questions* 14.7). But it was towards the end of the Empire that magic became widespread in Rome. J. R. Mozley writes: 'It is impossible to doubt that at this period attempts were made to injure enemies and to obtain private advantages through supernatural means, in such a way as to exhibit magic as a really malevolent, if not also a maleficent, practice' (Article on *Superstitio*, in W. Smith, *Dictionary of Greek and Roman Antiquities*). There are not a few sepulchral inscriptions which commemorate people whose death is said to have been compassed by magic. One of them reads: 'Eunia Fructuosa lies buried here. She died an undeserved death. Transfixed by spells she lay for a long time, so that her spirit was violently tortured out of her, before it was returned to Nature. The Shades or the heavenly gods will be the avengers of this crime' (*C.I.L.* 2756).

We may briefly look at some of these magical practices which would be among those which are forbidden by Paul. The name of the person to be injured was written on a tablet with sinister signs and words. A wax image of the person was made and then slowly melted down or destroyed in some other way (Virgil, *Eclogues* 8.80; Horace,

Satires 1.8, 32). Strips of lead were made with the name of the attacked person on them, and with a cursing prayer dedicated to the spirits of the underworld. The lead strip was then inserted into a tomb so that the spirits of the underworld would see it and act upon its curse. Bones were buried under a man's house to compass his death, as Tacitus tells was done in the case of the murder of Germanicus (Tacitus, *Annals* 2.69; Horace, *Satires* 2.8.22). Love philtres were common; astrology was rampant in an attempt to see into the future; there were perennial magical prescriptions for making gold out of base metals. Galen, the physician, condemns the folly of those who add sorceries and incantations to the use of herbs and drugs. That, he says, is not the practice of medicine (Galen, *De Simpl.* 6).

The evil eye was universally feared (Alciphron, *Letters* 1.15; Pliny, *Natural History* 7.16; Plutarch, *Symposium* 7). The evil eye was specially fatal to children. It could be guarded against by spitting into the folds of one's coat (Theocritus, *Idylls* 6.39; Pliny, *Natural History* 7.16). It could be guarded against by the use of amulets. Strangely enough, the amulet consisted of a little model of the *phallus* worn round the neck (*turpicula res*, Varro calls it: Varro, *Lingua Latina* 7.37). The same strange safeguarding amulet could be seen in gardens and on hearths (Pliny, *Natural History* 19.50).

The ancient world was riddled with magical practices. In Acts 19.19 we read of the magical experts of Ephesus who burned their books when they were converted by Paul's demonstrations of the power of the name of Jesus. How long this lasted and how serious a problem it was even in the Christian Church can be seen in the twenty-fourth canon of the Council of Ancyra in AD 314 or 315, in which it is laid down that 'those who practise divination, and follow the customs of the heathen, or who take men to their houses for the invention of sorceries, or for lustrations' must undergo 'five years of penance according to the established degrees'. It must have been quite extraordinarily difficult to root out from a superstitious world the practices which had become part and parcel of everyday life. And indeed some of the practices were not so much eliminated as Christianized, for we find Christians wearing round their necks, not now the ancient amulets, but Christian texts, and even little miniature copies of part of the NT, apparently manufactured for the purpose.

It may be that here is the best point at which to note a grim fact about the works of the flesh. Without exception, every one of them is a perversion of something which is in itself good. Immorality, impurity, licentiousness are perversions of the sexual instinct which is in itself a lovely thing and part of love. Idolatry is a perversion of worship, and was begun as an aid to worship. Sorcery is a perversion of the use of healing drugs in medicine. Envy, jealousy and strife are perversions of that noble ambition and desire to do well which can be a spur to greatness. Enmity and anger are a perversion of that righteous indignation without which the passion for goodness cannot exist. Dissension and the party spirit are a perversion of the devotion to principle which can produce the martyr. Drunkenness and carousing are the perversion of the happy joy of social fellowship and of the things which men can happily and legitimately enjoy. Nowhere is there better illustrated the power of evil to take beauty and to twist it into ugliness, to take the finest things and to make them an avenue for sin. The awfulness of the power of sin lies precisely in its ability to take the raw material of potential goodness and turn it into the material of evil.

ECHTHRA

AV, P: hatred; RV, RSV, W: enmity; NEB, M: quarrels; CKW: quarrelling. Other translations of other occurrences of the word —RSV: hostile or hostility (Rom. 8.7; Eph. 2.14, 16); M: feud (Eph. 2.16); W: mutual enmity (Eph. 2.16); P: conflicting elements (Eph. 2.14).

It is not necessary to spend any length of time discussing the meaning of *echthra*; *echthros* is the normal Greek word for an enemy, and *echthra* for enmity.

In the NT itself it occurs in only two other passages. In

Rom. 8.7 Paul writes that 'the mind that is set on the flesh is hostile to God', or, as the NEB better has it : 'The outlook of the lower nature is enmity with God.' And in Eph. 2.14, 16 it is used of the dividing wall of hostility which separates Jew and Gentile until both become one in Jesus Christ.

In the ancient world there were three kinds of enmities, and these enmities are still reproduced in life.

i. There was the enmity between class and class within the same city of the same country. Plato said that in every city there was a civil war between those who have and those who have not. There can be in any community a class warfare which it is not difficult for ill-disposed people to foment for their own malignant purposes.

ii. There was the enmity between Greek and barbarian. This, Plato said, was a war which knew no ending; and Isocrates pleaded that Homer should never be omitted from the educational curriculum of the Greek boy, because Homer shows the eternal breach between the Greek and the barbarian. To the Greeks there was in the literal sense a difference between the Greeks and the barbarians. 'There was,' writes T. R. Glover, 'some natural difference between Greek and barbarian. There was no thwarting Nature; and Nature had planned two distinct types of man—Greek and non-Greek—and the difference was fundamental' (T. R. Glover, *Springs of Hellas*, p. 32).

It is to be noted how essentially arrogant this Greek distinction was. A 'barbarian' was literally a man who said 'bar-bar', that is, a man who did not speak Greek. How, demanded Ctesias the ancient historian, can men who can only bark ever rule the world? Now this test, the test of Greek, relegated highly civilized nations, like the Egyptians, the Phoenicians, the Persians, the wealthy Lydians, to the rank of barbarian. Aristotle thought that the very climate of the world maintained this difference. Those who lived in the North in the cold lands had plenty of courage and spirit but little skill and intelligence; those who lived in the south in Asia Minor, as we now call it, in the warm lands had plenty of skill and intelligence and culture, but little spirit or courage. Only the Greeks lived in a climate designed by nature to produce the perfectly blended character (Aristotle, *Politics* 7.7.2).

To the Greek these 'barbarians' were by nature slaves, whom it was perfectly right for a superior Greek to reduce to servitude and to buy and sell. This attitude to the non-Greek comes out vividly in an adjective which Plutarch applies to Herodotus the ancient historian. Herodotus had an insatiable and what we might call an ecumenical curiosity. Great deeds to him were great deeds whether or not a Greek performed them. He was, as J. L. Myres writes of him in *The Oxford Classical Dictionary*, 'devoid of race prejudice and intolerance'. And the result is that Plutarch labels him with the word *philobarbaros*, lover of barbarians, as if the word were a condemnation (Plutarch, *De Mal. Her.* 857 A).

It is significant that two of the places in which this word *echthra* is used (Eph. 2.14, 16) refer to the relationship in the ancient world between Jew and Gentile. There was indeed a wall of hostility, an ancient feud, between Jew and Gentile. It was a hatred which existed on both sides. The Romans could speak of the Jewish religion as a barbarous superstition (Cicero, *Pro Flacco* 28), and of the Jewish people as the vilest of people (Tacitus, *Histories* 5.8). In the same passage Tacitus says of the Jews that they have an unshakable loyalty to each other, but a hostile hatred for all other men. Diodorus Siculus reports the saying that the Jews suppose all men to be enemies (31.1.1, 3). Apion declared that the Jews swore by the God of heaven and earth and sea never to show goodwill to a man of another nation, and especially never to do so to the Greeks (Josephus, *Against Apion* 1.34; 2.10). On the other hand, the Jews regarded the Gentiles as unclean. To intermarry with a Gentile was to be as good as dead. At their bitterest the Jews could consider the Gentiles as no better than unclean animals, hated by God, and destined to be fuel for the fires of hell. Anti-Semitism is no new phenomenon, and Jewish exclusiveness is of the essence of Judaism.

The iron curtain of racial prejudice and racial bitterness is no new thing. The spirit which produces racial riots and a colour bar is as old as civilization—and from the beginning it stands condemned in the Christian ethic and in the Christian faith.

iii. There is the enmity between man and man. In this case it is simplest to define *echthra* in terms of its opposite. *Echthra* is the precise opposite of *agapē*. *Agapē*, love, the supreme Christian virtue, is that attitude of mind which will never allow itself to be bitter to any man, and which will never seek anything but the highest good of others, no matter what the attitude of others be to it. *Echthra* is the attitude of mind and heart which puts up the barriers and which draws the sword; *agapē* is the attitude of heart and mind which widens the circle and holds out the hand of friendship and opens the arms of love. The one is the work of the flesh; the other is the fruit of the Spirit.

ERIS

AV: variance; RV, RSV, W: strife; NEB: a contentious temper; M: dissension; CKW: disputing; P: quarrelling. Other translations of other occurrences of the word—AV: debate (Rom. 1.29), contention (I Cor. 1.11); NEB: rivalry (Rom. 1.29); P: quarrelsomeness (Rom. 1.29), squabbling (I Cor. 3.3), argument (II Cor. 12.20).

It may be said that *echthra* and *eris* are very closely connected. *Echthra*, enmity, is a state and attitude of mind towards other people; and *eris*, strife, is the outcome in actual life of that state of mind.

Three times in Ecclesiasticus *eris* appears as one of the things which disrupt life. 'A hasty quarrel kindles fire, and urgent strife sheds blood' (Ecclus 28.11). Anger and envy, trouble and unrest, fear of death and fury and strife (Ecclus 40.5) are the ills of human life, as are death and bloodshed, strife and sword, calamities, famine, affliction and plagues (Ecclus 40.9).

In secular Greek *eris* is a vivid word. In Homer and Hesiod Strife is a grim goddess. Strife, rouser of hosts, Homer calls her (*Iliad* 20.48); he joins together Strife and Tumult and fell Death (*Iliad* 18.535). Hesiod tells how deadly Night bare Nemesis to affect mortal men, and after that Deceit and Friendship, hateful Age and hard-hearted Strife (Hesiod, *Theogonia* 225). To the Greeks Eris, goddess of Strife, was one of the malignant forces in life, producer of violence and of death.

Eris appears in primitive Greek science as one of the fundamental and essential and indestructible forces of the universe. All things, said Heraclitus of the natural processes of nature and the world, happen by strife and necessity (*Frag.* 215). And Aristotle writes of the views of Heraclitus: 'Heraclitus rebukes the author of the line, "Would that strife might be destroyed from among gods and men", for there would be no musical scale unless high and low notes existed, nor living creatures without female and male, which are opposites' (Aristotle, *Eudemian Ethics* 1235a25). It is the action and interaction between opposites which is of the very essence of nature, and, were it to cease, and were one element to become irresistibly dominant, then the universe would come to an end. Empedocles had the same view of the universe. Simplicius states his views thus: 'Empedocles makes the material elements four in number, fire, air, water and earth, all eternal, but changing in bulk and scarcity through mixture and separation; but his real first principles which import motion into these are Love and Strife. The elements are continually subject to an alternate change, at one time mixed together by Love, at another separated by Strife' (Empedocles, *Frag.* 426; Simplicius, *Phys.* 25, 21). So then for the Greek thinkers it may be said that strife is written into the structure of the universe. And it may be that that is why in secular Greek, at least in the earliest writers, *eris* is not altogether a bad word, but can describe the clash of mind with mind out of which true knowledge often comes, and the rivalry in honourable things which makes for excellence.

But in the NT itself *eris*, strife, is always an evil thing. In the thought of Paul there are two significant things about *eris*.

i. *Eris* is one of the evils which are characteristic of the pagan world (Rom. 1.29). The pagan world is a divided world; it is a world of broken and interrupted personal relationships, it is only in Christianity that there can be fellowship and unity in life. The Christian is forbidden to live in revelling and drunkenness, in debauchery and licentiousness, in strife and envying (Rom. 13.13). These are the things which a man must leave behind him when he becomes a Christian.

ii. But the really significant fact about Paul's use of the word *eris* is that four out of its six occurrences are connected with life in the Church. Three of them come from the Corinthian letters (I Cor. 1.11; 3.3; II Cor. 12.20). It is *eris* which divides the Corinthian church into sects and parties, claiming to be of Cephas, of Apollos, of Paul and of Christ. It is *eris* which has split the church, and which has brought enmity where there should be love. In the letter to the Philippians Paul writes that those who preach in unholy competition with himself, and whose preaching is at least as much directed towards discrediting Paul as it is to exalting Christ are preaching through *eris* (Phil. 1.15). Here we are coming to the meaning of *eris*. *Eris* invades the church and becomes characteristic of the church, when the leaders and the members of the church think more about people and about parties and about slogans and about personal issues than they do about Jesus Christ. Here is our warning. Whenever in a church Jesus Christ is dethroned from the central place, all personal relationships go wrong. When a man begins to preach, not to exalt Jesus Christ, but to exalt his own personal and private view of Jesus Christ, that is to say, when a man preaches a theology rather than a gospel, when a man begins to argue to demolish his opponent rather than to win him, then *eris* comes in.

No sin more commonly invades the Church than *eris*; none is more destructive of Christian fellowship; but *eris* cannot even gain an entry to the Church, if Christ be supreme there.

ZĒLOS AND PHTHONOS

Zēlos—AV: emulations; RV, RSV, M, W, P: jealousy; NEB: envy; CKW: rivalry.

Translations of *zēlos*, when it occurs in a good sense—Zeal: NEB, M, P (Rom. 10.2); AV, RSV (Phil. 3.6); RSV (II Cor. 7.7). Pious zeal: NEB (Phil. 3.6). Ardour: M (Phil. 3.6). Enthusiasm: P (Phil. 3.6; II Cor. 9.2). Fervent mind: AV (II Cor. 7.7). Eager to take my side or part: NEB, M (II Cor. 7.7). Keen interest on my behalf: P (II Cor. 7.7). Eagerness: NEB (II Cor. 7.11). Keenness: P (II Cor. 7.11).

Phthonos—AV, RV, W: envyings; RSV, M, CKW, P: envy; NEB: jealousies. Other translation of the word in another occurrence—jealous spirit: NEB (Phil. 1.15).

These words have to be taken together, because they so often occur together, and because there are cases in which the one has to be defined in contrast to the other. The broad principle which governs their meaning is that *zēlos* has a good and a bad sense, while *phthonos* is always bad.

i. We begin by taking the words as they occur in Scripture itself. *Zēlos* occurs in both senses in the Greek OT.

(a) In its good sense in the LXX *zēlos* is repeatedly used of God. The zeal of the Lord will perform this (Isa. 9.7). God has taken zeal as his whole armour (Wisd. 5.17). Here zeal is the unwearying determination of God to carry out his purposes and to vindicate his own. If we may express the matter in human terms, *zēlos* is the unflagging enthusiasm of God in working out his purpose in the world.

(b) *Zēlos* is the word which very frequently expresses the holy jealousy of God. There is a picture which we meet again and again in the prophets; it is the picture of Israel as the bride of God. When, therefore, Israel strays away from God and worships other gods, Israel may be said to give herself to other lovers who are false lovers; and in such a situation the prophets speak of the jealousy of God who is the true husband of Israel (Ezek. 16.37, 38; 23.25). The jealousy of God is the jealousy of a lover whose loved one is being foolishly false.

(c) As *zēlos* is used in a good sense of God, so it can be used in a good sense of men. The Psalmist says: Zeal for thy house has consumed me (Ps. 69.9). My zeal, he says, consumes me (Ps. 119.139). This zeal is the passion for God which burns a man up, and sets him aflame for God.

(d) But equally in the Greek OT *zēlos* has a bad sense, the sense of an envy and a jealousy which are destructive of personal relations and of individual happiness. Eliphaz tells Job: 'Wrath destroys the foolish one, and envy slays him that has gone astray' (Job 5.2). Jealousy makes a man furious (Prov. 6.34). The writer of Ecclesiastes takes the cynical view that toil and diligence are simply the outcome of a man's envy of his neighbour (Eccles. 4.4). Love, hatred and envy, all perish in death (Eccles. 9.6). Jealousy and anger shorten life, and anxiety brings on old age too soon (Ecclus 30.24). *Zēlos* can be an evil thing and a wrecker of life.

ii. Let us now turn to the NT. In Paul's letters *zēlos* occurs nine times, no fewer than six times in a good sense. The Jews have a zeal for God, even if it is not enlightened (Rom. 10.2). Paul in his zeal for the law was a persecutor of the Church (Phil. 3.6). Paul speaks of the longing and the zeal of the Corinthians for himself (II Cor. 7.7), and of the zeal which their repentance had produced in them (II Cor. 7.11). He speaks of the zeal of the Corinthians in their contribution to the collection for the poor of the Jerusalem Church (II Cor. 9.2). He is jealous for the Corinthians for it was he who betrothed them as a bride to Christ (II Cor. 11.2). On the other hand strife and envying are two of the things of which the Christian must rid himself in view of the nearness of the coming of Christ (Rom. 13.13). Jealousy and strife are the proof that the Corinthians are still under the domination of their lower nature (I Cor. 3.3). Jealousy is one of the errors which Paul fears to find if he returns to Corinth (II Cor. 12.20). Here then is this word, balanced, as it were, between good and evil.

iii. When we turn to the examination of the use of these two words in secular Greek there is real help in the definition of their meaning. Three writers are particularly helpful.

(a) In Plato the two words are repeatedly used together. Anger, fear, yearning, mourning, love, jealousy (*zēlos*) and envy (*phthonos*) are pains of the soul (*Philebus* 47 E). A community in which there is neither wealth nor poverty is the only community in which insolence and injustice, rivalries and jealousies, receive no chance to flourish (*Laws*

679 C). As soon as there is wealth there are jealous looks (*Republic* 550 E). But there is one usage in Plato which is specially significant. After the success of Athens against the barbarians, and after the way in which Athens saved Greece, she had to undergo the inevitable penalty of success. First she was assailed by jealousy (*zēlos*), and then by envy (*phthonos*) which brought war in its train (*Menex.* 242 A). From here it is clear that Plato regarded *zēlos* as a stage on the way to *phthonos*. *Zēlos*, we might say, is the envy which casts grudging *looks*; *phthonos* is the envy which has arrived at hostile *deeds*. There is, as we shall see, a further difference; but this much is established, *zēlos* is less serious, less bitter, less malignant than *phthonos*; *phthonos* is that in which *zēlos* can culminate, unless the heart be cleansed.

(b) Aristotle actually deals most lucidly with the difference between the two words. For Aristotle *zēlos* is a good and a necessary feeling of the soul. *Zēlos* is emulation; it is the feeling which comes to a man when he sees some one else in possession of some noble thing. That feeling is not sorry that the other person possesses the fine thing; it is sorry that it itself does not. It is a virtue and characteristic of the virtuous man. There is no grudging in it; but there is the spur to a noble ambition to possess a virtue which has been glimpsed but not possessed. On the other hand, *phthonos* is 'a kind of pain at the sight of good fortune', 'pain at another's good,' as the Stoics defined it (Diogenes Laertius 7.63, 111). And this pain springs not from the fact that the beholder does not possess the fine thing; it springs from the fact that the other person does. The man who has *phthonos* in his heart is not fired with noble ambition; he is simply embittered at the sight of someone else possessing what he has not got, and he would do his utmost, not to possess the thing, but to prevent the other person from possessing it. *Phthonos* is base, and the characteristic of the base man (Aristotle, *Politics* 2.10, 11). *Zēlos* can be noble ambition; *phthonos* can never be anything else but ill-natured and embittered jealousy. Xenophon in the *Memorabilia* hands down a definition of *phthonos*. 'It is a kind of pain, not at a friend's misfortune, nor at an enemy's good fortune. The envious are those who are annoyed only at their friends' successes' (Xenophon, *Memorabilia* 3.9.8). *Phthonos* is an ugly thing.

(c) Plutarch does much to define the meaning of these words. *Zēlos*, he writes, is the desire to emulate what we commend; it is the eagerness to do what we admire, and not to do, and not even to tolerate, what we censure. It is the imitation (*mimēsis*) of that which is excellent. Love for a person, he says, cannot be really active, unless there is some jealousy (*zēlos*) in it. Real love of virtue cannot be effective unless it creates in us, not envy (*phthonos*), but emulation (*zēlos*) in honourable things. It is not contentiousness; it is rivalry in goodness (Plutarch, *Progress in Virtue* 14). On the other hand, *phthonos* envies all prosperity and all success. It is, therefore, illimitable, 'being like ophthalmia, troubled at everything bright'. *Phthonos* is annoyed at prosperity. Insects attack ripe corn, and envy attacks the good and those who are growing in virtue and in repute (Plutarch, *On Envy and Hatred* 2-8). Envy, said Euripides, is the greatest disease amongst men.

We may see the difference between the two emotions, as Plutarch and Aristotle saw them, in two Greek stories. Themistocles was unable to rest when he thought of the mighty victory that Miltiades had won at Marathon; the thought of it filled him with a noble ambition; and he never rested until he had set his victory at Salamis beside the victory of Miltiades at Marathon. He did not grudge Miltiades his greatness; he desired to do something that was like it (Plutarch, *Themistocles* 3). That is *zēlos*. Aristides was called the Just. He was on trial, and a man came to him, not knowing who he was, and asked Aristides to write his vote for his own banishment, because he could not write himself. 'What harm has Aristides done you?' Aristides asked. 'I am tired,' said the man, 'of hearing him called the Just' (Plutarch, *Aristides* 7). This was no noble ambition to be like greatness; it was simply the embittered resentment that anyone should be great. That is *phthonos*.

Phthonos does not occur in the canonical OT at all. It does occur in the Apocrypha. 'Through the devil's envy death came into the world, and those who belong to his party experience it' (Wisd. 2.24). Envy is a devilish thing. 'Neither will I travel in the company of sickly envy, for envy does not associate with wisdom' (Wisd. 6.23). In I Maccabees the historian says of the Romans: 'They trust one man each year to rule over them and to control all their land. They all heed this one man, and there is no envy or jealousy among them' (I Macc. 8.16). *Phthonos* is clearly a hateful thing.

Paul has it only twice. In Rom. 1.29 it is one of the sins which are characteristic of the heathen world. And in Phil. 1.15 it is the moving spirit of those who preach Christ, not so much to win people for Christ, as simply to spite Paul. They do not so much covet his success for themselves, as they wish to deny it to him.

The pagan writers would have allowed some necessary greatness to *zēlos*, as rivalry in noble ambition, but the day was to come when Clement of Rome was to trace all sin to this very quality. Envy (*zēlos*), he wrote to the Corinthians, was responsible for the murder of Abel by Cain, for the flight of Jacob before Esau, for the selling of Joseph into Egypt by his brothers, for Saul's attempted murder of David, and for the pagan hatred which shed the blood of the Christian martyrs (*I Clement* 4-6).

There is something of the tragedy of the human situation here. *Phthonos* was always an ugly word, but *zēlos* could denote a great thing which had degenerated into a sin. Maybe it is true to say that there is no better test of a man than his reaction to the greatness and to the success of some one else. If it moves him to the *zēlos* which is noble ambition to goodness, that is the work of the Spirit, but, if it moves him to a bitter and envious resentment, that is the work of the flesh, and what ought to be a spur to goodness has become a persuasion to sin.

THUMOS

AV, RV: wrath; RSV: anger; NEB: fits of rage; M: temper; W: outbursts of passion; CKW, P: bad temper. Other translations of other occurrences of the word—fury: RSV (Rom.

2.9); angry tempers: NEB (II Cor. 12.20); ill-feeling: P (II Cor. 12.20); passion: NEB (Eph. 4.31); furious rage: P (Col. 3.8).

Thumos is a word with an almost unlimited potentiality for good and for evil. It can describe a quality without which no good character can flourish; it can describe a quality which is the wrecker of personal relationships, and the destruction of fellowship within the community.

i. Let us begin by looking at *thumos* in the Greek OT, in which it occurs more than three hundred times.

(a) In the LXX *thumos* can be used of *men in a bad sense*. Cain departed from wisdom in anger, and through it became his brother's murderer (Wisd. 10.3). Pride was not created for men, nor fierce anger for those born of women (Ecclus 10.18). Jealousy and anger shorten life, and anxiety brings on old age too soon (Ecclus 30.24). There is no venom worse than a snake's venom and no wrath worse than an enemy's wrath (Ecclus 25.15).

(b) In the LXX *thumos* can be used of *men in a good sense*. Three things move the sage to anger: A warrior in want through poverty, intelligent men who are treated with contempt, a man who turns back from righteousness to sin (Ecclus 26.28). There the word means righteous indignation in face of that which is wrong.

(c) In the LXX *thumos* is more than once used of *wild animals*. The wise man knows the nature of animals and the temper of wild beasts (Wisd. 7.20). Wisdom speaks of beasts full of rage, and of the terrible temper of wild beasts (11.18; 16.5). *Thumos* is in fact, as we shall see, the only possible word for the rage of an animal.

(d) In the LXX *thumos* is used of *God*. Mercy and wrath are with him, and his *anger* rests on sinners (Ecclus 5.6). Men are warned to think of God's wrath, and of the day of death (Ecclus 18.24). In the NT, especially in the Revelation, *thumos* is used of the wrath of God. Sinners will be compelled to drink the cup of the fury (*thumos*) of God's wrath (Rev. 19.15; 16.19; cp. 14.19; 15.1; 16.1). In the Revelation *thumos* is not only used of God, it is also used of the devil. The devil comes in wrath, because he knows that his time is short (12.12).

Quite clearly *thumos* is a word with a wide range of meaning, including wrath human and divine, wrath devilish and beastly, wrath noble and destructive.

ii. Let us now turn to *thumos* in the secular Greek writers. In these writers we shall again see how *thumos* is a quality which is, as it were, always poised upon a razor's edge.

(a) *Thumos* can be a noble word. In Aristotle it often means spirit, not in the religious sense of the term, but in the sense in which we speak of a vital and virile person being spirited. It is classed with courage (*Nicomachean Ethics* 116b23). It is the capacity of the soul whereby men love, whereby they have the power to command, whereby they thrill to freedom, whereby they are righteously indignant at the sight of wrong. It is the commanding and the indomitable element in the soul (*Politics* 7.6.3). No soul, writes Plato, can stand against wrong without noble passion (*thumos*) (*Laws* 731 B). It is the word that Xenophon uses in the phrase strength and *courage* (*Cyropaedia* 4.2.21). Clearly, here we have a word which can describe a quality of the soul on which strength and gallantry and chivalry and leadership depend.

(b) But the classical writers are in no doubt at all in regard to the peril which lurks in *thumos*. It is like an explosive which can equally well be used to blast a way through obstacles in the way or to blast a town into ruins. Aristotle uses it for what in English we would call passion (*Nicomachean Ethics* 111b11). An action produced by *thumos*, he said, cannot be held to be due to malice aforethought; if due to a fit of passion (*Nicomachean Ethics* 135b26). Plato, as we have seen, says in *The Laws* that no soul can stand for the right without *thumos*, but he immediately goes on to say that by this same *thumos* murder can be done, and that to be kept in its rightful place it must be disciplined and chastised (*Laws* 867 B, D). The Platonic Definitions have it that *thumos* is 'a violent impulse without reason' (415 E). Aristotle will not have this; he will not totally divorce *thumos* and reason; but he has a vivid picture. 'Anger,' he says, 'does hear reason, but it hears it wrongly, like a servant who dashes out of the room, before his master's order is completed' (*Nicomachean Ethics* 149a3). *Thumos* is a great quality, but *thumos* needs a strong leash.

(c) The nature of *thumos* for good and for evil may best of all be seen from the derivation which the Greeks attached to it. Aristotle speaks about 'the heat and swiftness of its nature' (*Nicomachean Ethics* 1145b31). The Greeks derived it from the verb *thuein* which means *to boil*. '*Thumos* has its name,' Plato writes, 'from raging and boiling of the soul' (Plato, *Cratylus* 419 E). Basil, using another metaphor, describes it as 'intoxication of the soul'.

Now this is the very quality which gives *thumos* its special characteristic, and which distinguishes it from the word *orgē*, which is usually translated *wrath*. *Orgē* is, for instance, Paul's word for the wrath of God. The characteristice feature of *thumos* is that it is very violent but very brief. Jeremy Taylor called *thumoi* (the plural) 'great but transient angers'. The Stoics defined *thumos* as anger beginning (Diogenes Laertius 7.63), in contrast to *orgē*, which Cicero in Latin defined as *ira inveterata*, anger which has become inveterate (Cicero, *Tusc. Disp.* 4.9). Ammonius said that *thumos* is *proskairos*, temporary, momentary, while *orgē* is *poluchronōs*, *mnēsikakia*, longlasting cherishing of the memory of evil. *Thumos*, the Greeks said, was like fire in straw, quickly blazing up and just as quickly burning itself out.

Thumos is, therefore, not long cherished anger; it is the blaze of temper which flares into violent words and deeds, and just as quickly dies.

iii. Finally, we look at *thumos* as Paul uses the word. In Rom. 2.8 he uses it of the anger of God. Wrath (*orgē*) and fury (*thumos*) awaits the disturbers of the peace. He fears that he may find *thumos* in the distressed and disturbed church at Corinth (II Cor. 12.20). Bitterness and wrath, anger and clamour, slander and malice are to be quite put away (Eph. 4.31). Anger, wrath, malice, slander, foul talk are the sins of the heathen, and a Christian must eliminate them from his life (Col. 3.8). *Thumos*, the explosive temper, is something which must be banished from the Christian life.

Many a person is well aware that he has a violent temper; and many a person claims that he cannot help it, and expects others to accept and to forgive his bursts of passion. The NT is quite clear that such displays of temper are sinful manifestations that a man is still in the grip of his own lower nature. It may well be that such a person is never fully aware of the way in which he wounds others and produces a situation in which fellowship becomes very difficult. Because he blazes and forgets he thinks that others should equally be able to forget the pain he has inflicted. Let such a person remember that such displays of temper are sin, and that the way to overcome them is through the power of the Spirit in his heart.

At the same time no one would wish to banish anger from life. There are two sayings in the NT. There is the saying of Jesus : 'I say to you that everyone who is angry with his brother shall be liable to judgment' (Matt. 5.22). (The saving clause 'without a cause' is not in the best MSS., and is rightly omitted by the newer translations such as the RSV, and the NEB.) On the other hand, Paul writes : 'Be angry, but do not sin' (Eph. 4.26). Wherein lies the antiseptic which turns the strong poison of anger into a useful medicine? The broad answer is simply this—anger which is selfish, and which comes from pride, and undue sensitiveness to one's own feelings is always and invariably wrong; anger for the sake of others, anger which is cleansed of self, can often be a weapon to be used by God.

ERITHEIA

AV : strife; RV : factions; RSV, CKW : selfishness; NEB : selfish ambition; M, P : rivalry; W : intrigues. Other translations of other occurrences of the word—contention : AV (Rom. 2.8; Phil. 1.17); personal rivalry : NEB (II Cor. 12.20; Phil. 1.17); divided loyalties : P (II Cor. 12.20); partisanship, the partisan spirit : RSV (Phil. 1.17), P (Phil. 1.17); for their own ends, for private ends : M (Phil. 1.17; 2.3).

The many and varied translations of this word show the

uncertainty of its meaning. Its general meaning is plain enough. It describes a wrong attitude in the doing of work and in the holding of office. In secular Greek the word and the corresponding verb had two uses.

i. *Erithos* is a day-labourer, *eritheuesthai*, the verb, is to work for hire, and *eritheia* is working for hire. The word can be used in that sense with no ill meaning at all. We read, for instance, in Tobit, that Anna *earned money* at women's work (Tob. 2.11). All the words are simply connected with working for pay.

But, it is not a very great step from working for pay to working *only* for pay, working with no other motive than to see how much one can make. The word therefore can describe the attitude of the man who has no regard for service, no pride in craftsmanship, no joy in work, and who is only in any piece of work for what he can get out of it.

ii. In Aristotle the word *eritheuesthai*, the verb, acquires another meaning. Perhaps again the meaning is not absolutely clear, but again the general atmosphere is clear. In Aristotle the word comes to mean canvassing for office by means of hired partisans, and Aristotle lists this activity as one of the practices which in the end lead to revolutions. Rackham translates it 'election intrigue'. At the back of this there is something of the same idea as attaches to the first meaning of the word. The political action described is the action of a man whose sole motive is either party or personal ambition, and who does not seek office with the high desire to serve the state and the community and his fellow-men, but who only seeks to gratify his personal ambition, his personal desire for power, or the exaltation of a party in competition with other parties and not for the good of the state. The word describes the attitude of the man who is in public service for what he can get out of it, only this time the motive is not so much material or financial gain as it is personal prestige and power. Burton translates the word by the general phrase 'selfish devotion to one's own interest'. Lightfoot translates the word more narrowly 'caballings'.

Paul uses the word four times. In Rom. 2.8 he speaks of those who are *ex eritheias*, those who are dominated by *eritheia* and who do not obey the truth, and he contrasts them with those who by patience in well-doing seek for glory and honour and immortality, and it is quite clear that it is not human glory and honour which are in question. In II Cor. 12.20 he uses it of the sins which he fears to find in Corinth and joins it with quarrellings, jealousies, anger, slander, gossip, conceit and disorder. In Phil. 1.17 he uses it of those in whose proclamation of the gospel the main motive is competition with himself, those whose preaching is more to frustrate him than it is to exalt Christ. In Phil. 2.3 he urges the Philippians to do nothing from *eritheia* or conceit, but in humility to count others better than themselves and then there follows the great passage which tells how Jesus Christ emptied himself of his glory for men.

These usages are significant for fixing the meaning which Paul attached to the word. It is to be noted that three out of the four instances occur in contexts in which the main problem lies in competing parties within the Church. The Corinthian church was split into competing parties; in the Philippian church preaching had become a means of belittling Paul rather than of proclaiming Christ. In Paul the word clearly denotes the spirit of personal ambition and rivalry which issues in a partisanship which sets a party above the Church.

Such a motive would be bad enough in the world, but for such a motive to invade the Church is tragedy. And yet in fact it does. There are those whose work in the Church is designed to exalt their own prominence and importance, and who are bitterly disappointed when they do not receive the place and the honour which they believe they have earned. There are those, cruel as it may seem to say so, who serve on committees and boards because these are the one place in the world where they can succeed in being someone. Their apparent voluntary service is a means of gratifying a desire for power.

Further, there are those in the Church, the worst type of ecclesiastics, who do in fact plan and intrigue in support of a policy and a line; and it may well happen that they are more concerned to secure the triumph of their policy than to secure the general welfare of the Church. It is not impossible to hear lengthy debates in the courts of the Church in which the concern is not with the mission of the Church so much as it is with the triumph of some party or policy or even person within the Church.

There is one answer to all this. So long as Christ is in the centre of the life of the individual and of the Church *eritheia*, personal ambition and partisan rivalry, can never even begin to appear; but when Christ is removed from the centre and when any man's ambitions and policies become the centre, then inevitably and certainly *eritheia*, personal competition, will invade the Church and will disturb the peace of the brethren.

DICHOSTASIA

AV: sedition; RV: divisions; RSV, NEB, W: dissension; M, P: factions; CKW: party spirit. Other translations of the other occurrence of the word in Rom. 16.17—NEB: quarrels; P: those who cause trouble.

Dichostasia is not a common word either in biblical or in secular Greek. It only occurs once again in Paul's writings in Rom. 16.17 in which Paul warns the Roman Christians to avoid those who create *dissensions* and difficulties. In the LXX it occurs only in I Macc. 3.29 where it describes the national dissension and unrest which followed reckless new legislation which was a violent break with the past. Herodotus uses it of the resulting situation when one of two commanders changed sides in the middle of a campaign (Herodotus 5.75). Obviously such an action would cause an acute state of division. Plato quotes a saying of Theognis that in the days of *dichostasia* a faithful man is worth his weight in gold (Plato, *Laws* 630 A; Theognis 5.77, 78). The word denotes a state of things in which men are divided, in which feuds flourish, and in which unity is destroyed.

Dichostasia bears its picture on its face; it literally means 'a standing apart', that is, a state in which all community, all fellowship, and all togetherness are gone. It is all too obvious that such a state is tragically common among men.

There is *personal* division; there can arise situations in which two people have come to a stage when they neither meet each other or speak to each other. Even the work of a church can be rendered difficult by feuds between its members.

There is *class* division; there are indeed political faiths which are based on nothing short of the necessity of class warfare. There is still the necessity to learn the practical wisdom of the words of Jesus: 'Every kingdom divided against itself is laid waste, and no city or house (NEB, household) divided against itself will stand' (Matt. 12.25). United we stand, divided we fall, is a truth which is never out of date.

There is *party* division. Macaulay looked back on the great days of the Roman Republic when 'none was for a party and all were for the state'. One of the saddest sights in modern democratic party government is to see party politics manœuvring to make capital out of national danger or misfortune, and acting as if national welfare was a pawn in the game of party ambition and party politics.

There is *racial* division. There are still societies from which a man may be excluded because of the colour of his skin. There are few words which are a greater negation of the Christian ethic than the word *apartheid*.

There is *theological* division. The *odium theologicum*, theological hatred, is no new thing. There is no realm of thought more prone to fix labels on people than theology is, and to regard as a heretic the man who wears the wrong label.

There is *ecclesiastical* division. It may well be that the greatest problem which the Church at present faces is the problem of her own disunity, and that disunity may well be not only the Church's greatest problem, but also the Church's greatest sin. Kagawa, the great Japanese Christian, was deeply distressed by this disunity. Once he said: 'I do not speak English very well, and sometimes when I say the word *denomination* people think that I have said *damnation*—and to me they are the same thing.'

There is here a challenge and a summons, not so much to criticize others as to examine ourselves. There is nothing easier than to confuse prejudices with principles, and to confuse unreasonable stubbornness with unwavering resolution. It is perfectly true that often a Christian has to stand alone, but a man will do well to examine himself when he finds that the opinions he holds are separating him from the community of which he forms a part. He may be right, but it is a grave responsibility to be a cause of division in any church or community. Before he separates himself from others a man ought to remember the solemn words of Cromwell to the intransigent Scots: 'I beseech you by the bowels of Christ, think it possible that you may be mistaken.'

HAIRESIS

AV, RV: heresies; RSV, M, P: party spirit; NEB: party intrigues; W: factions; CKW: party quarrels.

The English word heresy is to all intents and purposes a transliteration of the Greek word *hairesis*. In English, heresy is a word with a distinctively bad meaning; it denotes a belief which is contrary to orthodoxy and to true doctrine. But in Greek *hairesis* is not necessarily a bad word for it means either an act of choosing or a choice.

In the Greek OT it can be used for instance of the choice of a gift as an offering to God (Lev. 22.18); and it can be used of a purpose or a plan, a chosen course of action. In the LXX it is said that Symeon and Levi accomplished their iniquitous *purpose* (Gen. 49.5).

In the NT by far most commonly it denotes a body of people belonging to a particular school of thought and action and holding a particular kind of belief, as, we might say, a body of people who have all made the same choice. So it is used in the sense of a party, as of the party of the Pharisees (Acts 15.5; 26.5); the Sadducees (Acts 5.17); the Nazarenes (Acts 24.5); and twice of the Christians (24.14; 28.22). In such cases it is commonly translated sect, but there is no necessary implication that the sect is what we would now call an heretical sect; it is simply a body of people who have chosen the same way of belief and life.

When *hairesis* reaches this stage of meaning, human nature being what it is, its further degeneration becomes wellnigh inevitable, for it then comes to mean a choice of belief, and perhaps also of conduct, which separates a man from the community of which he is a part; it is then that the word comes to mean heresy in the modern sense of the term.

In this passage it is not heresy which is so much in question as division within the Church into groups and cliques and parties, by which the togetherness of the Church is destroyed. The most significant usage of the word is in I Cor. 11.19. There Paul is rebuking the Corinthian Christians for their conduct at the Lord's Table. In the ancient Church two things were combined; there was the *Agapē*, or Love Feast, and the sacrament of the Lord's Supper itself. The Love Feast was a very beautiful part of the life of the early Church. It was a common meal to which Christians came together on the Lord's Day. To see the picture correctly we have to remember that at this stage the Church had no buildings of its own, and that the Christian groups met in the rooms of ordinary houses. To this common meal everyone brought what he could, and it was shared in loving fellowship together. Very probably in many cases this would be the only decent meal that a slave ate in the course of the week. In Corinth, instead of sitting down as one, sharing united fellowship, the members of the group were divided into cliques and sections, *haireseis* (the plural form of the word), and, instead of sharing all they had in a common stock, each little group within the group kept to itself what it had brought, and the result was that some had far too little and some had far too much. What should have been one harmonious, sharing, loving unity was broken up into little self-contained, selfish, exclusive fragments. This is what Paul calls *hairesis*. It is the breaking up of the unity of the Church into cliques who shut their circle to all but their own number.

A fragmented Church is not a Church at all; a group whose circle is closed is certainly not a Christian group. If anyone regards his social status as something which shuts him off from others of a different social status, then he has not begun to see even the first meaning of Christianity. There is all the difference in the world between believing that we are right and believing that everyone else is wrong. Unshakable conviction is a Christian virtue; unyielding intolerance is a sin. There are many more roads to God than the road by which we have come.

Here again we are presented with the same warning and the same challenge. No one will deny that the Church owes much to those who had the courage and the conviction to stand alone; but the fact remains that a man must closely examine himself, if he finds that his so-called piety and his chosen belief are separating him from his fellow-men, for Christianity was not meant to divide men but to unite them, and, if we claim the right to choose for ourselves, we must concede that same right to others. Christian love must still be able to love those with whose belief and conduct it cannot agree.

METHĒ AND KŌMOS

Methē—AV, RSV, RV, CKW, P: drunkenness; NEB, M: drinking bouts; W: hard drinking.
Kōmos—AV, RV: revellings; M: revelry; RSV: carousing; NEB, P: orgies; W: riotous feasting; CKW: disorderly dancing. Other translation of the other occurrence of the word in Rom. 13.13—AV: rioting.

It is natural to take these two words together. In the one other place in which they occur in the NT (Rom. 13.13), they again occur together, where revelling and drunkenness are two of the things which the Christian must for ever lay aside.

The attitude of the ancient world, and of the greater part of Scripture, to wine and such drinks is quite clear. The practice of the ancient world and of Scripture abhorred drunkenness and regarded drunkenness as utterly shameful, but it hardly occurred to it either to enjoin or to practise total abstinence. In the Greek world even the child drank wine; breakfast was, for instance, simply a slice of bread dipped in wine. The Pithoguia, the festival of the wine harvest, in Greece was a festival in which all of all ages participated. Yet in Greece there was very little drunkenness, for the normal practice was to drink wine in a very diluted form, two parts of wine to three parts of water.

The danger of drunkenness is fully recognized in the LXX. The writer of the Proverbs has it: 'Wine is an intemperate thing and strong drink is full of violence' (Prov. 20.1). The prophets express the condemnation of those who have 'staggered through drunkenness' (Isa. 28.7; Ezek. 23.33; 39.19). In Tobit we read: 'What you hate do not do to anyone. Do not drink wine to excess, or let drunkenness go with you on your way' (Tob. 4.15). But on the whole the attitude of the ancient world and of the biblical writers to wine is shown in the words of Ben Sirach: 'Wine is as good as life to a man, if it be drunk moderately; what life is then to a man without wine? for it was made to make men glad. Wine measurably drunk and in season bringeth gladness to the heart and cheerfulness to the mind; but wine drunken with excess maketh bitterness of the mind, with brawling and quarrelling. Drunkenness increaseth the rage of a fool till he offend; it diminisheth strength and maketh wounds' (Ecclus 34.27-30). We know that Jesus was no ascetic for John can tell the story of the changing of the water into wine (John 2.1-11), and his enemies could fling their taunt and slander at him that he was a gluttonous man and a wine-bibber.

It may well be argued that total abstinence is a Christian duty, but it cannot be argued on the strength of definite statements and prohibitions in Scripture. It has to be argued on the strength of the great principle which Paul twice lays down: 'It is right not to eat meat or drink wine or do anything that makes your brother stumble' (Rom. 14.21). Christian liberty is never to become a stumbling-block to the weak. 'Therefore, if food is a cause of my brother's falling, I will never eat meat, lest I cause my brother to fall' (I Cor. 8.9, 13). The argument cannot be based on definite injunctions of Scripture; only on the principle that it is not right to claim permission to indulge in any pleasure which can be the ruin of someone else.

Kōmos is revelry, but in secular Greek it has a particular background to it. It particularly described the joyful procession through the streets and the subsequent celebration following a man's victory in the games. His friends united to convoy him through the streets and then to feast and drink in celebration. In secular Greek it has the meaning which the English word 'celebration' can on occasion have.

But in biblical Greek *kōmos* is a much more serious word. It does not occur anywhere else in the NT except in Romans 13.13. It does not occur in the canonical books of the Greek OT, but it occurs twice in the Apocrypha. In Wisdom it is used in a passage about the increasing sin of mankind. They came to slay their children in sacrifice, to use secret ceremonies, to make *revellings* of strange rites. 'They kept neither lives nor marriages any longer undefiled; but either one slew another traitorously, or grieved him by adultery' (Wisd. 14.23, 24). In a context like that it is clear that this word means far more than an occasional celebration which might run into a temporary excess. But the really significant use of the word is in II Macc. 6.4. The passage tells of the actions of Antiochus Epiphanes. Antiochus in the early part of the second century BC invaded Jerusalem. He made a quite deliberate attempt to wipe out the Jewish faith. It was a crime punishable by death either to keep the Sabbath or to possess a copy of the Law. He defiled the great altar of the burnt-offering by offering swine's flesh on it, and he turned the rooms in the Temple courts into public brothels. The Temple, it says, was filled with riot and *revelling*. *Kōmos* expresses a lustful excess in physical and sexual pleasure which is offensive to God and to man alike. It may well be that the best translation of it is that of J. W. C. Wand, when he translates it debauchery.

These two words, drunkenness and revelry, *methē* and *kōmos*, describe the pleasure which has become debauchery. There is one way for the Christian to avoid all such pleasure. It is simply to remember that he is for ever in the presence of Jesus Christ, and so to seek ever to make life in its work and in its pleasure fit for Jesus Christ to see.

III

THE FRUIT OF THE SPIRIT

AGAPĒ

The Greatest of These

T H E necessary aim of every writer on the ethics of the good life is to paint in words the portrait of the good man. To put it in another way, the continuous task of the ethical teacher is to set out the various ingredients in the recipe of goodness. That is what Paul does in Galatians 5.22, 23 when he lists the great qualities in the fruit of the Spirit— love, joy, peace, patience, kindness, goodness, faithfulness, gentleness, self-control.

It is inevitable that love should stand at the head of the list, for God is love (I John 4.8), and, therefore, necessarily the greatest of these is love (I Cor. 13.13). Love is the bond of perfection, the perfect bond, that which binds everything together in a perfect harmony (Col. 3.14), and love is in itself the fulfilling of the law (Rom. 13.10).

We must begin by defining our terms. There are times when English, as compared with Greek, is a poverty-stricken language. It is said that, in Gaelic, if a lad loves a lass there are twenty different ways in which he may tell her so! In English there is but one word for to love, and that word must do duty for many feelings. But Greek has four words for to love.

(i) There is the word *erōs*. This is characteristically the word for love between the sexes, for the love of a man for a maid; it always has a predominantly physical side, and it always involves sexual love. Aristotle says that *erōs* always begins with the pleasure of the eye, that no one falls in love without first being charmed by beauty, and that love is not love, unless one longs for the loved one when absent, and eagerly desires his presence (Aristotle, *The Nico-*

machean Ethics 9.4.3). Epictetus describes this kind of love as a passionate compulsion (*Discourses* 4.1.147). This word does not appear in the NT at all, not because the NT despises or rejects physical love, but because by NT times this word had come to be connected with lust rather than with love. *Erōs*, as it has been put, is love still unconverted.

(ii) There is the word *philia*. This is the highest word in secular Greek for love. It describes a warm, intimate, tender relationship of body, mind and spirit. It includes the physical side of love, for the verb *philein* can mean to kiss or to caress, but it includes very much more. And yet even in this word there is something lacking. 'Love is not love,' said Shakespeare, 'which alters when it alteration finds.' But *philia*, like all human things, can alter. Aristotle writes: 'The lover's pleasure is in gazing at his beloved, the loved one's pleasure is in receiving the attentions of her lover, but when the loved one's beauty fades, the friendship (*philia*) sometimes fades too, as the lover no longer finds pleasure in the sight of his beloved, and the loved one receives no attention from the lover' (Aristotle, *The Nicomachean Ethics* 8.4.1). It is true that *philia* describes the highest kind of human love, but it is also true that the light of *philia* can flicker and its warmth grow cold.

(iii) There is the word *storgē*. This is the word which is most limited in its sphere, for in secular Greek this is the word of family love, for the love of the parent for the child and the child for the parent, for the love of brothers and sisters and of kith and kin.

(iv) There is the word *agapē*. Here we have little guidance from secular Greek. In secular Greek the corresponding verb *agapan* is common enough, but the noun *agapē* hardly occurs at all. As R. C. Trench has it: '*Agapē* is a word born within the bosom of revealed religion.' Nor is this accidental. *Agapē* is a new word to describe a new quality, a word to describe a new attitude to others, an attitude born within the Christian fellowship, and impossible without the Christian dynamic.

How, then, are we to determine the meaning of *agapē*? We can determine its meaning best from the way in which

AGAPĒ 65

Jesus himself speaks of it. The basic passage is Matt. 5.43-48.
There Jesus insists that human love must be patterned on
the love of God. And what is the great characteristic of the
love of God? God sends his rain on the just and on the unjust, and makes his sun to rise on the evil and on the good.
Therefore, the meaning of *agapē* is unconquerable benevolence, undefeatable goodwill. *Agapē* is the spirit in the heart
which will never seek anything but the highest good of its
fellow-men. It does not matter how its fellow-men treat it;
it does not matter what and who its fellow-men are; it does
not matter what their attitude is to it, it will never seek
anything but their highest and their best good. Immediately
this is seen certain vital truths emerge.

(i) When Aristotle writes of love, his whole attitude is
that only he who is deserving of love can be loved. He
speaks of those who wish to be loved, the desire that love
should be reciprocated, and he says of people who have this
desire that their desire is ridiculous, if they have nothing
attractive about them (Aristotle, *The Nicomachean Ethics*
8.8.6). He insists that a man cannot expect to be loved, 'if
there is nothing in him to arouse affection' (*The Nicomachean Ethics* 9.1.2). Epictetus says much the same, when he
says: 'Whatever a man is interested in, he naturally loves'
(*Discourses* 2.22.1). Plato said: 'Love is for the lovely.' But
the distinguishing quality of Christian love lies precisely in
its obligation and its ability to love the unlovely and the un-
lovable, to seek the man's highest good quite independently
of what the man is, or is doing, or has done. In Christian
love the idea of merit has passed out of sight.

(ii) For the Greek writers love is almost necessarily an
exclusive thing. Aristotle defines love as 'friendship in a
superlative degree'. He goes on to say that, if that is so, it
can be for one person, and for one person only (Aristotle,
The Nicomachean Ethics 9.10.5). It is in fact the conviction
of Aristotle that love cannot be diffused, nor can friendship
be widely spread. In friendship the circle must be narrow;
in love there is not even a circle, only one point on which
everything is focused. Christian love is the very reverse of
that. It is an all-embracing benevolence. Augustine said of
God that God loves us all as if there were only one of us

C

to love; and Christian love must be modelled on the love of God.

(iii) There is one sense in which Christian love differs radically from ordinary human love. Ordinary human love is a reaction of the heart; it is something which simply happens. We use the phrase 'falling in love'. Ordinary human love is something with the creation and dawn of which we have nothing to do. But *agapē*, Christian love, is an *exercise of the total personality*. It is a state not only of the heart but also of the mind; it is a state not only of the feelings and the emotions but also of the will. It is not something which simply happens and which we cannot help; it is something into which we have to will ourselves. It is not something with which we have nothing to do; it is a conquest and an achievement. It has indeed been said that in at least one of its aspects *agapē* is the ability and the power and the determination to love the people we do not like. It is certainly true that this Christian love is not an easy sentimental thing; it is not an automatic and unsought emotional response. It is a victory won over self. The plain fact is that this Christian love is the fruit of the Spirit; it is something which is quite impossible without the dynamic of Jesus Christ. That is why it is futile to talk about the world accepting the ethics of the Sermon on the Mount and of Christian love. The plain truth is that the world cannot accept them; only the Spirit-filled, Christ-devoted Christian can.

(iv) There was a large area of pagan thought to which this idea of Christian love was a revolutionary contradiction of all that it had aimed at. All the philosophies contemporary with Christianity had one aim and object; the one thing which they all sought was peace of mind, *ataraxia*, serenity, tranquillity, the heart at rest. In order to attain to that they all in one form or another insisted on the utter necessity of two basic qualities. The first was *autarkeia*, which means absolute self-sufficiency, absolute independence of anything or anyone outside oneself. *Autarkeia* is the attitude of mind which finds its happiness and its peace entirely and exclusively within itself. The second was closely allied with that; it was *apatheia*. *Apatheia* is not apathy in the sense of indifference; *apatheia* is essential inability to feel joy or sorrow, gladness or grief; it is the attitude of mind and heart which cannot be touched by anything that can possibly happen to itself or anyone else. It is the heart insulated from all feeling and from all emotion. If this is the ideal of life, then quite clearly the great enemy of peace is love; love is the great disturber. Epictetus tells how Caesar has brought political peace and safety to this world, and then he says despairingly: 'But can Caesar give us peace from love?' (Epictetus, *Discourses* 2.13.10). He agrees that a man should become affectionate (*philostorgos*), but only in such a way that he will never at any time become dependent on anyone else for his happiness and joy, for, if a man allows anyone to enter his heart and to dwell there, freedom is gone for ever (Epictetus, *Discourses* 3.24.58). To Epictetus love is a kind of slavery (Epictetus, *Discourses* 4.17.57). For that reason philosophy is a training in the attainment of indifference. Epictetus insists that men should never set their hearts on anyone or anything, for nothing and no one must be necessary to us. A man must teach himself not to care. Let him begin with trifling and unimportant things—a pot, a cup which can in any event be easily broken. Let him go a little further on to a tunic, a paltry dog, a mere horse, a bit of land. If anything happens to any of these things, let him teach himself not to care. Then in the end he will gradually reach a stage when he will not care what happens to his own body, when he can lose his children, his wife, his brothers—and not care (Epictetus, *Discourses* 4.1.110, 111).

It is quite true that sometimes Marcus Aurelius speaks in an apparently different way. Love the men among whom your lot is cast, he says, and love them wholeheartedly. Love mankind and follow God. All that is rational is kin, and it is part of man's nature to care for all men. The deity enthroned within us cherishes a fellow-feeling for men. If you cannot convert the evildoer, then remember that kindliness was given to you to meet such a case and to treat such a man. No one must ever wrest kindliness from us. We must live in gentleness to those who endeavour to stand in our way and to those who are a thorn in our side (Marcus Aurelius, *Meditations* 6.38; 7.31, 34, 36; 9.11; 11.9). The true Cynic will necessarily be flogged, and, even while he is being flogged, he must love the men who flog him, as though he were the father or brother of them all (Epictetus, *Discourses* 3.22.55).

But, in seeking the meaning and significance of passages such as these, it must always be remembered that this attitude to others was born, not of identification with others, not of sympathy with others, not of sharing in their human situation, but from conscious superiority. The wise man was so armoured in his virtue, so above ordinary little men, that he would never allow the antics and the foolishness of lesser mortals to impinge on his Olympian calm.

In direct contrast to this, *Christian love is caring*. Christian love is the very reversal of the first principles of pagan philosophy. The pagan philosopher said: 'Teach yourself not to care.' The Christian message said: 'Teach yourself to care passionately and intensely for men.' The pagan philosopher said: 'You must not on any account allow yourself to become personally and emotionally involved in the human situation.' The Christian message says: 'You must so enter into the human situation that you see and think and feel with the other person's eyes and mind and heart in your deep identification with others.' The Christian message offered the way to happiness in that very attitude which the pagan philosopher regarded as the way to unhappiness. For the Christian the principle at the heart of life was the one thing which the pagan philosopher sought entirely to eliminate from life.

Let us then analyse the meaning of this *agapē*, using in particular the material in the letters of Paul in which the word occurs more than sixty times.

(i) Everything begins with the love of God, for God is the God of love (II Cor. 13.11). Christian love is the reflection of God's love, and from God's love it draws its pattern and its power. This love of God is *a completely undeserved love*, for the proof of it is that it was while we were still sinners that Christ died for us (Rom. 5.8). The New Testament could never countenance any view of the Atonement which implied or suggested that anything that Jesus did changed or altered the attitude of God towards men, that somehow Jesus changed the wrath of God into the love of God. The whole process of salvation takes its beginning in the undeserved love of God. Further, God's love is *a productive and transforming love*. It is that love of God which, poured into men's hearts, produces the great qualities of Christian life and character (Rom. 5.3-5). There is a human love which saps a man's moral fibre, which paralyses his effort, and which withdraws him from the battle of life; but the love of God is the transforming dynamic of the Christian life, begetting in a man the patience, the endurance, the experience, the hope which arm him for life. God's love is *an inseparable love*. There is nothing in time or in eternity which can separate a man from it (Rom. 8.35-39). Here indeed is one of the great arguments for life after death. Love is the perfection of relationship between two personalities, and God's love offers a relationship with himself which in the very nature of things nothing can break or interrupt. God's love is quite simply *a great love* (Eph. 2.4-7). And, according to this passage, God's love is a great love for three reasons. First, it loved us when we were dead in sins. Second, it quickened us to newness of life. Third, it surpasses time, and goes beyond life into the heavenly places.

(ii) As Paul speaks of the love of God, so he also speaks of the love of Jesus Christ. For Paul the love of God and the love of Jesus Christ are one and the same thing. In Rom. 8.35-39 Paul begins by asking, Who shall separate us from *the love of Christ*? And he ends by saying that nothing can ever separate us from *the love of God* which is in Christ Jesus our Lord. To Paul, Jesus *is* the love of God in demonstration and in action. Paul goes on to say certain things about the love of Jesus Christ.

It is a love *which passes knowledge* (Eph. 3.19). Love is always a mystery. Any man who is loved is left in wondering amazement that it should be so. The love of Christ is not so much something to be explained, as it is something before which a man can only wonder and worship and adore. The love of Jesus Christ is *the pattern of the Christian life*. The Christian must walk in love as Christ loved him (Eph. 5.2). The love of Christ is the pattern of the personal relationships of the Christian. The love of Christ is *the controlling dynamic of the Christian life*. It is the love of Christ which controls him (II Cor. 5.14). The Christian is not hounded to goodness by fear; he is lifted to goodness by the obligation of love which wakens the sleeping chivalry in the soul.

(iii) One of Paul's most consistent connections is the connection of *love and faith* (Eph. 1.15; Col. 1.4; I Thess. 1.3; 3.6; II Thess. 1.3; Philemon 5). The highest praise which Paul can give to any church is to say that its members have *faith* in Christ and *love* for one another. Christianity involves a double personal relationship and a double commitment, a relationship and a commitment to Christ, and a relationship and commitment to men. Christianity is communion with God and community with men. 'No man,' said John Wesley, 'ever went to heaven alone.' 'God,' said the wise old counsellor to Wesley when he was contemplating withdrawal from the world, 'knows nothing of solitary religion.'

There is a double connection between faith and love. In Eph. 6.23 Paul prays that his people may have *faith with love*; and in Gal. 5.6 he speaks of faith working through love, or, as it perhaps may be better translated, faith energized, set in action, by love. We may put it in this way —love without faith is sentimentality, and faith without love is aridity. Love must be based on faith. It is, for instance, unquestionably true that the only true basis for a belief in democracy is the belief that all men are the children of God; and the only true basis of evangelism is the theological conviction that Christ died for all men. Faith must be set on fire by love, lest it becomes intellectualism, and lest the theologian should become, as Anatole France had it, a man who has never looked out of the window.

This combination of faith and love must produce action, for love must never be merely a pose (Rom. 12.9). It is perfectly possible to preach love and to live a loveless life, to sing the praise of love in words and to deny the fact of love in deeds. In particular love will produce two things. It will produce *practical generosity*. When Paul was taking the collection for the poor Christians of Jerusalem, his repeated appeal to the younger churches is to show the sincerity of their love, to provide the proof of their love by their Christian generosity (II Cor. 8.7, 8, 24). It will issue in *forgiveness*. When the troubles at Corinth had ended, and when peace was restored, it is Paul's appeal to the Corinthians that they should reaffirm their love by forgiving the man who had been the storm-centre of all the trouble (II Cor. 2.8).

Faith must be joined to love and love to faith, and that combination must issue in the generous hand and the forgiving heart.

We must now go on to see, as we might put it, this basic Christian quality of love in action in the Christian life.

(i) Love is *the atmosphere of the Christian life*. The Christian, says Paul, must walk in love (Eph. 5.2). Every life carries its own atmosphere with it. One of her pupils said of the great American teacher Alice Freeman Palmer : 'She made me feel as if I were bathed in sunshine.' On the other hand, Richard Church in his autobiographical essay tells of the first day that he went to school. He was aware of what he called 'a cold impersonal pretence of benevolence in the air'. There is an atmosphere which is like a warm cloak and an atmosphere which is like a cold douche. The Christian carries this atmosphere of radiant benevolence wherever he goes. Paul puts this same truth in another way. Love, he says, is *the garment of the Christian life*. It is his charge to the Colossians that they should put on love (Col. 3.14). We speak of a person being clothed in beauty, or armoured in virtue. The Christian life is clad in this outgoing goodwill to all men.

(ii) Love is *the universal motive of the Christian life*. 'Let all things be done in love,' Paul writes to the Corinthians (I Cor. 16.14). The Sermon on the Mount leaves us in no doubt as to the importance of the motives of the heart in the Christian life (Matt. 5.21-48). There is a kind of generosity whose main motive is the gaining of prestige. There is a kind of warning and rebuke which springs from a delight in hurting and in seeing people wince. There is even a kind of toil and service which spring from pride.

One of the great neglected duties of the Christian life is self-examination, and maybe self-examination is neglected because it is so humiliating an exercise. If we examine ourselves we may well find that there is hardly anything in this world which we do with motives which are pure and unmixed. Even if that is so, we must still hold up before ourselves the standard by which we ought to live, the insistence that the only Christian motive is love.

(iii) Love is *the secret of Christian unity*. Christians are knit together in love (Col. 2.2). The significant thing about this Christian love is that it goes out in ever-expanding circles. (a) It begins by being *love of the saints*, that is, love for the other members of the Christian fellowship, love for our fellow-Christians (Eph. 1.15; Col. 1.4; I Thess. 3.12). (b) It is love for the leaders of the Church (I Thess. 5.12, 13). It is a simple fact that the only gift that Paul ever asked from his churches was that they should pray for him, that they should hold him on their hearts, and bear him in their hands in prayer (Rom. 15.30). (c) It ends by being love for all men. Christians are to increase in love to each other, and to all men (I Thess. 3.12). There is a kind of Christianity which is summed up in the four lines of doggerel:

> We are God's chosen few,
>   All others will be damned;
> There is no room in heaven for you—
>   We can't have heaven crammed.

Christian love is the reverse of that; it expands until it seeks to enfold the whole wide world in its arms, and to receive all men into its heart.

(iv) There are three closely related spheres within which this Christian love operates.

(a) Love is *the accent of Christian truth*. The Christian must necessarily be a lover of the truth (II Thess. 2.10), but at all times he must speak the truth in love (Eph. 4.15). It is easy to speak the truth in such a way that it hurts and wounds; it is not impossible to find pleasure in seeing some one wince and quiver under the lash of truth. 'The truth,' said the Cynics, 'is like the light to sore eyes.' Florence Allshorn was the famous and much loved Principal of a great women's missionary college. Inevitably there were times when she had to rebuke her students; but, it was said of her that, when she had cause to rebuke, she always did so as if with her arm round the person to be rebuked. Truth spoken to hurt can produce nothing but resentment; but truth spoken in love can waken the penitence which is a saving thing.

(b) Love is *the ground of Christian appeal*. When Paul is pleading with Philemon on behalf of the runaway slave Onesimus, it is to love that he appeals (Philemon 7). It is to love that Paul appeals when he asks for the prayers of the Roman church before he sets out for Jerusalem (Rom. 15.30). The Christian will never resort to force; the Christian will seldom appeal to his authority. The weapon of the Christian is always love's appeal and seldom power's demand.

(c) Love is *the motive of Christian preaching*. Even in its sternest moments the motive and accent of the words of Jesus is love. It is in love that he yearns over the city wherein he is to die (Matt. 23.37). Maybe the most misunderstood chapter in the Bible is Matthew 23 in which there is the terrible series of Woes directed against the Scribes and Pharisees. It is common to think of that chapter, and to read that chapter, as if it had been spoken in a blazing passion of white hot anger, and as if Jesus had been lashing these people with the whip of his tongue. 'Woe unto you!' says Jesus (Matt. 23.13 ff.). But the word in the Greek is *Ouai*, and the very sound of it is a lament. Alas for you! says Jesus, Alas for you! This is not the accent of passionate anger; it is the accent of heart-broken love.

There are times when certain preachers give the impression that they hate their hearers, and they assail them with such a battery of threats that it almost sounds as if they would be glad to see them damned. It is on record that once, when a man was asked why he had ceased to attend a certain church, he answered: 'I was tired of having handfuls of gravel thrown in my face every Sunday.' Men can be wooed into accepting the gospel far more readily than they can be scolded into accepting it. Stanley Jones in his book on Conversion tells of the work of Dr Karl Menninger of the Menninger Clinic, Topeka. The whole work of the clinic was organized round love. It was taken as a principle that 'from the top psychiatrists down to the electricians and caretakers, all contacts with patients must manifest love'. And it was 'love unlimited'. The result was that hospitalization time was cut in half. There was a woman who for three years sat in her rocking-chair and never said a word to anyone. The doctor called a nurse and said: 'Mary, I'm giving you Mrs Brown as your patient. All I am asking you to do is to love her till she gets well.' The nurse tried it. She got a rocking-chair of the same kind as Mrs Brown's, sat alongside her, and loved her morning, noon and night. The third day the patient spoke and in a week she was out of her shell—and well.

Stanley Jones quotes certain other examples of this principle at work. Father C. Hilmer Myers speaking of gangland boys said: 'Such boys can be reached by giving them what they crave most—love from an adult ready to help in an emergency.' A Hindu manufacturer told Stanley Jones why he had come to one of his Ashrams: 'Do you know why I have come? Years ago when I was a boy we heckled a missionary preaching in the bazaar—threw tomatoes at him. He wiped off the tomato juice from his face and then after the meeting took us to the sweetmeat shop and bought us sweets. I saw the love of Christ that day, and that's why I'm here.' An old negro said of a younger negro who had got himself into bad trouble: 'You have just to love him out of it.' There was an habitual drunkard in the community. One morning he said: 'The boys rocked me last night.' His friend replied: 'Maybe they were trying to make a better man out of you.' The man said: 'Well, I never heard of Jesus throwing rocks at a man to make him better.' Men can be won far more by loving them into heaven than by trying to threaten them out of hell.

(v) Love is *the controller of Christian liberty*. Christian liberty is to be used, not as an excuse for licence, but as an obligation to serve one another (Gal. 5.13). There are many things which for the stronger brother are perfectly safe, and which he could perfectly legitimately allow himself;

but he abstains from them because he loves, and refuses to injure by his example, the weaker brother for whom Christ died (Rom. 14.15). If love is the basis of life, then responsibility is the key-note of life. No Christian thinks of things only as they affect himself. The privilege of Christian liberty is conditioned by the obligation of Christian love.

(vi) This Christian love is no easy and sentimental emotion. Love is *clear-sighted*. It is Paul's prayer for the Philippians that their love may abound in all knowledge and in all sensitive awareness, and that it may enable them to distinguish between the things which differ, and so to choose the right (Phil. 1.10). With Christian love there enters into life a new sensitiveness to the feelings and the needs and the troubles of others, a new awareness of goodness, and a new horror of sin. So far from being blind, Christian love teaches a man to see with a vividness and to feel with an intensity which he never experienced before.

In the same way Christian love is *strong*. In Paul's correspondence with the church at Corinth there are two most illuminating uses of the word love. In II Cor. 2.4 Paul writes of the stern and severe letter which he had already sent to the Corinthian church, a letter which had caused the Corinthians grief and pain. But, he says, that letter was written, not to cause them grief and sorrow, but to prove his love to them. The very last sentence of the first letter to the Corinthians is: 'My love be with you all!' (I Cor. 16.24). The letters to Corinth are far from being sentimental letters. They administer discipline; they convey rebuke; they do not hesitate to threaten to use the chastening rod; they deal out the sternest correction; they even demand the ejection of the trouble-maker from the fellowship of the Church—and yet they are the outcome of love.

Love in the NT sense of the term never makes the mistake of thinking that to let a person do as he likes is to love him. The NT is clear that there are times when anger, discipline, rebuke, punishment and chastening are parts of love.

(vii) It is easy to see that the acquirement and the practice of Christian love are no easy task. In I Cor. 14.1, Paul uses a most significant expression. The AV translates it:

'Follow after charity.' But the verb which is translated *follow after* is *diōkein* which means *to pursue*. Christian love is not something which simply happens; it is something which has to be sought, desired, pursued, something into which a man must pray and discipline himself. So far from being an automatic possession, it is the supreme achievement of life.

It may even be said that Christian love is not only difficult; it is humanly speaking impossible. Christian love is not a human achievement; it is part of the fruit of the Spirit. It is shed abroad in our hearts by the Holy Spirit.

And so we come to the final truth about this Christian love. There is a magnificent verse in the Letter to the Philippians. In it the word love does not itself appear, but the idea is the idea which is at the heart of Christian love. Paul writes, as the AV has it: 'I long after you all in the bowels of Jesus Christ' (Phil. 1.8). Literally that means: 'I love you with the very love of Christ. Through me and in me Christ is loving you. The love which I bear to you is none other and nothing else than the love of Christ himself.'

And so in the end we can only say that Christian love springs to life when Christ is incarnated again in a man who has given himself absolutely to him.

CHARA

The Joy of Living

It is only when we study it in detail that we discover what a book of joy the New Testament is. In the New Testament the verb *chairein* which means *to rejoice* occurs seventy-two times, and the word *chara* which means *joy* occurs sixty times. The New Testament is the book of joy.

The normal Greek greeting both in speech and in letters is the word *chairein*, and it is usually translated simply 'Greetings!'. It is so used in the letter to Felix about Paul of the Roman officer Claudius Lysias (Acts 23.26). If we were to give *chairein* its full and literal translation, it would be: 'Joy be with you!', and there are certain occasions in the New Testament when only the full translation will do.

When the Christian Church decided at the Council of Jerusalem that the door of the Church was to be opened to the Gentiles, the leaders of the Church sent to the Gentile Christians in Syria and Antioch and Cilicia a letter informing them of that great decision, and the letter begins: '*Chairein*. Joy be with you!' (Acts 15.23). The door to Christian joy was open. When James was writing to the Christians scattered throughout the world, and when he was thinking of them as the exiles of eternity, he begins his letter: 'Joy be with you!' (James 1.1). Almost the last word that Paul wrote to his friends at Corinth was: 'Joy be with you, brothers!' (II Cor. 13.11). There are two very beautiful uses of this word *chairein* in connection with the life of Jesus. When the angel came to Mary, to tell her of the child whom she was to bear, his greeting was: 'Joy be with you!' (Luke 1.28). And on the Resurrection morning the greeting of the Risen Christ to the women who had come to mourn was: 'Joy be with you!' (Matt. 28.9). This great greeting, 'Joy be with you!' rings triumphantly through the pages of the New Testament. So, then, let us examine this Christian joy as the New Testament tells us of it.

(i) We must begin by noting that joy is *the distinguishing atmosphere of the Christian life*. We may put it this way—whatever be the ingredients of the Christian life, and in whatever proportions they are mixed together, joy is one of them. In the Christian life joy always remains a constant. 'Rejoice in the Lord,' Paul writes to his Philippian friends, and he goes on to repeat his command: 'Rejoice in the Lord always; again I will say, Rejoice' (Phil. 3.1; 4.4). 'Rejoice always,' he writes to the Thessalonians (I Thess. 5.16). It has been said that 'Rejoice!' is the standing-orders of the Christian.

In the letter to the Colossians there is a very significant passage. Paul tells the Colossians that he is praying for them, and that he is asking God that they should be filled with all knowledge of God's will in all spiritual wisdom and understanding, so that they may live a life worthy of the Lord, fully pleasing to him, bearing fruit in every good work, and increasing in the knowledge of God. Then he goes on : 'May you be strengthened with all power, according to his glorious might, for all endurance and patience'— and then there come the final words 'with joy' (Col. 1.9-11). Every virtue and all knowledge is to be irradiated with joy; even the patience and the endurance which might well be bleak and grim things are to be lit with joy. 'The kingdom of heaven,' Paul wrote to the Romans, 'is righteousness and peace and joy' (Rom. 14.17).

There is no virtue in the Christian life which is not made radiant with joy; there is no circumstance and no occasion which is not illumined with joy. A joyless life is not a Christian life, for joy is the one constant in the recipe for Christian living.

When we examine the references to joy in the New Testament in all their variety and their multiplicity, they fall into a certain pattern, and they tell us of certain spheres in which the Christian joy is specially to be discovered.

(a) There is *the joy of Christian fellowship*. The New Testament is full of the simple joy of what can best be called 'togetherness'. It is a joy even *to see* such fellowship. Paul writes to Philemon to tell him what joy and comfort he has received from the sight of Philemon's love and from the sight of the way in which the saints have been refreshed by Philemon's loving care (Philemon 7). In the famous saying the heathen looked at the Christian Church and said, 'See how these Christians love one another.' It must never be forgotten that one of the greatest evangelizing influences in the world is the sight of true Christian fellowship, and one of the greatest barriers to evangelism is the sight of a church in which fellowship has been lost and destroyed. It is a still greater joy *to enjoy* Christian fellowship. It rejoices Paul's heart that his Philippian friends have remembered him with gifts (Phil. 4.10). To see Christian fellowship is great, to be wrapped around in it is greater yet. It is a joy *to see Christian fellowship restored*. When Titus came back from the troubled church at Corinth with the news that the breach was healed and fellowship restored, then Paul rejoiced (II Cor. 7.7, 13). It is a joy to *experience Christian fellowship reunited*. The New Testament knows the simple joy of meeting friends again. John trusts that he will meet his friends again, and then his joy will be complete (II John 12).

In the New Testament there is nothing of that religion so-called which isolates a man from his fellow-men. The New Testament vividly knows the joy of making friends and keeping friends and reuniting friends, for friendship and reconciliation between man and man are the reflection of fellowship and reconciliation between man and God.

(b) There is *the joy of the gospel*. There is *the joy of the new discovery*. It may be said that the gospel story begins and ends in joy. It was tidings of great joy that the angels brought to the shepherds (Luke 2.10), and the wise men rejoiced when they saw the star which told them of the birth of the king (Matt. 2.10). So in the beginning there was joy. On the Resurrection morning the women returned from the tomb and from their encounter with the Risen Lord in fear and great joy (Matt. 28.8). The disciples could scarcely believe the good news for very joy (Luke 24.41). When Jesus came into the midst of them the disciples were glad when they saw the Lord (John 20.20). And at the very end, as Luke tells the story, after the Ascension, the disciples returned to Jerusalem with great joy (Luke 24.52). The gospel story begins, continues and ends in joy.

There is *the joy of receiving the gospel*. It was with joy that Zacchaeus received Jesus into his house (Luke 19.6). The Thessalonians received the word with joy (I Thess. 1.6). Repeatedly Acts tells of the joy which came to men when the gospel arrived in their midst. Philip's preaching brought joy to Samaria (Acts 8.8); after his baptism the Ethiopian eunuch went on his way rejoicing (Acts 8.39). There was joy in Antioch of Pisidia when the Gentiles heard that the gospel was to leave the synagogue and come out to them (Acts 13.48). The New Testament makes it clear that conversion should be one of the happiest experiences in all the world.

There is *the joy of believing*. It is Paul's prayer for the

Christians at Rome that the God of hope will fill them with all joy and peace in believing (Rom. 15.13). It is the joy of their faith that Paul wishes to increase for the Philippians (Phil. 1.25). The New Testament makes it clear that Christian belief is followed by Christian joy. It was said of Burns that he was haunted rather than helped by his religion. There have always been those who have made an agony of their religion. But for the New Testament belief and joy go hand in hand.

There is *a certain sternness* in this Christian joy. It is a joy which rejoices even *in discipline and in testing*. James bids his readers to count it all joy when testing comes (James 1.2). The Christian joy is like the joy of a woman whose travail has passed and whose child has come (John 16.21, 22).

It is a notable thing how often in the New Testament *joy and affliction walk hand in hand*. In spite of persecution the Christians in Antioch are filled with the Holy Spirit and with joy (Acts 13.52). The Christian may be sorrowful but he is also rejoicing (II Cor. 6.10). The gospel brought tribulation to Thessalonica but it also brought joy (I Thess. 1.6).

This joy in tribulation can be a very wonderful thing, and its wonder lies in the fact that it is endured and undertaken for Jesus Christ. Peter and John left the Sanhedrin and its threats rejoicing that they were counted worthy to suffer for the name of Jesus (Acts 5.41). Peter encourages his people by telling them that when they suffer they are sharing the sufferings of Christ himself (I Peter 4.13).

The most startling passage in the New Testament is in Col. 1.24 where Paul says that he rejoices in his sufferings. 'In my flesh,' he says, 'I complete what is lacking in Christ's afflictions for the sake of his body, that is, the Church.' How can there be anything lacking in the sufferings of Jesus Christ? How can anyone in any sense complete what is lacking in the sufferings of Christ? Let us take an analogy. It may be that in his laboratory or his operating theatre or his research room a scientist or a surgeon or a physician toils and sweats and labours and suffers and endangers and risks and destroys his own health to find some cure or some help for the pains and ills of men. But that discovery remains useless until it is taken out from the laboratory and made available for men all over the world. And it may well be that those who take it out to men have to sweat and toil and suffer and sacrifice to make it available. And it may accurately and fitly be said that their sufferings to make the gift available to men fill up and complete the sufferings of the great man who made the original discovery. The work of Jesus Christ is done and completed. But it has still to be made known to men. Time and time again in history men have laboured and suffered and died to tell men of that which Jesus Christ did for them. And in their sufferings they may well be said to be completing the sufferings of Jesus Christ himself. Here is the great uplifting thought that, if ever our loyalty to Jesus and our service of him cost something, it means that we to are completing the sufferings of Jesus Christ. What higher privilege could there be than that? If this is so, it is true that ours is a joy which no man taketh from us (John 16.22).

(c) There is *the joy of Christian work and witness*. There is joy in *the sight of God in action*. The Seventy returned with joy, because the devils were vanquished at the name of Christ (Luke 10.17). At the sight of Jesus' wonderful works people rejoiced because of the glorious things that were done by him (Luke 13.17; 19.37). There is joy in *the sight of the spread of the gospel*. Barnabas was glad when he saw the Gentiles gathered in at Antioch (Acts 11.23). The tale of the spread of the gospel brought great joy to the brethren (Acts 15.3). The gospel is the last thing which any Christian wants to keep to himself. The further it spreads and the more who share it, the greater his joy. There is the joy of the teacher and the preacher in *the Christian progress of his people*. The news of the obedience of the Christians in Rome has spread abroad and Paul is glad on their behalf (Rom. 16.19). The unity of the congregation is the joy of the pastor (Phil. 2.2). Even in his absence Paul rejoices at the steadfastness of the Christians at Colossae and the progress of the Christians at Thessalonica (Col. 2.5; I Thess. 3.9). John rejoices when his children walk in the truth (II John 4). 'No greater joy,' he says, 'can I have than this, to hear that my children follow the truth' (III John 4).

It must never be forgotten that, as the New Testament sees it, *the object of all Christian preaching is to bring men joy*. 'These things have I spoken to you,' said Jesus, 'that my joy may be in you, and that your joy may be full' (John 15.11). Jesus' object in speaking to his disciples was that they might have his joy fulfilled in themselves (John 17.13). John's aim in writing to his people was that his and their joy might be complete (I John 1.4). It is Paul's desire for the Corinthians that he may work with them for their joy (II Cor. 1.24). Paul would wish to be spared for a little while longer that he may help the Philippians in their progress and joy in the faith (Phil. 1.25).

It may be that a preacher has to awaken sorrow and penitence in his people; it may be that he has to awaken fear within their hearts; it may be that he has to rouse them to self-loathing, and to humiliation. But no Christian sermon can ever end there. The sermon which leaves a man in dark despair is not a Christian sermon, for after the shame and the humiliation of penitence there must be the joy of forgiveness claimed and the love of God experienced. No man should ever rise from a Christian service without the possibility of joy flaming and blazing before him. Stanley Jones tells of Rufus Moseley 'the most bubbling Christian' he ever knew. Someone said of him: 'The first time I heard him I thought he was crazy, but the second time I heard him I knew he was crazy.' Someone once asked Mosely if he thought that Jesus ever laughed. 'I don't know,' he said, 'but he certainly fixed me up so I can laugh.'

It may be that in the end of the day the greatest of all will be *the joy in the people whom we have brought to Jesus Christ*. To Paul it is the Philippians and the Thessalonians who are his joy and his crown (Phil. 4.1; I Thess. 2.19, 20). The writer to the Hebrews urges those who are set in leadership and authority to be so faithful to their trust that they may render account at the end of the day not with grief but with joy (Heb. 13.17).

When Samuel Rutherford was lying in gaol for his faith,

his mind went back to the little parish of Anwoth where he had lived and ministered and worked. He was thinking of the people he had taught and loved there and he was thinking of the end which he could not now escape. Mrs Cousins puts his thoughts at that moment into words :

> Fair Anwoth on the Solway
>   To me thou still art dear;
> Ev'n from the verge of heaven
>   I drop for thee a tear.
> O if one soul from Anwoth,
>   Shall meet me at God's right hand,
> My heaven will be two heavens
>   In Emmanuel's land.

And so we come to the end, for this joy is nothing other than the joy of God, for the joy of God is the joy of one who finds things which have gone lost, like the shepherd and the lost sheep (Luke 15.5, 7; Matt. 18.13); like the joy of the woman who found the coin that was lost (Luke 15.10); like the joy of the father whose lost son came home (Luke 15.32).

For man and God alike the greatest of all joys is the joy of love reborn and love restored, and the joy of the pastor in his people is nothing other than the joy of God.

EIRĒNĒ

Life at its Best

There were few things for which the ancient world longed so wistfully as it longed for peace. The search for peace was the universal search. The aim of all the ancient philosophies was *ataraxia*, serenity, tranquillity, the quiet mind. Caesar might be able to produce a world at peace, but what men longed for was a heart at peace, a peace not of Caesar's proclamation but of God's (Epictetus, *Discourses* 2.13.12). In this search for peace there are certain ideas which keep recurring.

(a) Peace can only come with the elimination of desire. 'If you wish to make Pythocles happy,' said Epicurus, 'add not to his possessions, but take away from his desires.' Nothing that you could give a man could give him peace. You must take from him these instinctive human desires which make of life a frustration and a battleground.

(b) Peace can only come with the death of emotion. A man must make himself *apathēs*, emotionless. If he gives anyone his heart to keep, if he allows anyone to have the keys to his inmost being, then peace is lost for ever. As Glover had it, these thinkers made of life a desert and called it a peace.

(c) Peace comes from the acquisition of indifference. In this life everything may be included in one of two classes. There are the things which are in a man's control and there are the things which are not. The only thing which is in a man's control is his mind, his moral choice, the attitude which he will take to life and to circumstances. To every external thing, to everything which can be affected by forces and circumstances outside his control, a man must preserve an absolute indifference. Caring for any person or any thing must be strangled before it is born, so the Stoics taught.

(d) Peace comes from complete self-sufficient independence, from *autarkeia*. A man must never become in any sense dependent on anything outside himself. His happiness must never depend on anything outside himself. His life must be absolutely self-contained, defended by the determination not to care.

These were the basic ideas of peace, 'absence of pain in the body or trouble in the mind', as Epicurus called it. It is quite clear that these ancient philosophers saw peace in terms of detachment, self-isolation, insulation against life. The one forbidden thing was involvement in the human situation as it existed outside oneself. And it is quite clear how different that is to the New Testament way of life and to the Christian ideal. Let us then look at the New Testament idea of peace.

The word *peace* came into the New Testament with a

great history. It is the translation of the Hebrew word *shalōm*. It is true that *shalōm* means *peace*, and it is by *peace* that it is mainly translated in the AV, although it is also translated *soundness* of body (Ps. 38.3). *welfare* (Gen. 43.27), *prosperity* (Job 15.21). *Shalōm* really means *everything that makes for a man's highest good*, all that makes life life indeed. In English *peace* has come to have something of a negative meaning. It is apt to mean the absence of war and the absence of trouble. For instance, if in a campaign hostilities actually came to an end and there was no more fighting we would be likely to say that there was peace; but quite certainly the Hebrew would not call a situation where there was a blasted earth, and where people still regarded each other with a kind of terrified suspicion, peace. In Hebrew though peace is something much more positive; peace is everything which makes for a man's highest good. The greeting *salaam* does not simply express the negative wish that a man's life may be free from trouble; it expresses the positive hope and prayer that he may enjoy all good gifts and blessings from the hand of God. In thinking of the meaning of peace, both in the Old and the New Testament, it is essential to bear in mind the positive meaning of the word.

Let us then briefly look at this word *eirēnē* as it is used in the LXX.

i. It describes the serenity, the tranquillity, the perfect contentment of the life which is completely happy and completely secure. The way of righteousness will be peace, and the effect of righteousness will be quietness and assurance for ever (Isa. 32.17). The Psalmist will lie down in peace and sleep, for it is God who makes him to dwell in safety (Ps. 4.8). Jeremiah contrasts the land of peace with the swelling of the Jordan (Jer. 12.5). The word has in it the calm and the serenity of the life from which fear and anxiety are banished for ever.

ii. *Eirēnē* is the great word to describe the perfection of relationships.

(a) It is the word of human friendship. A man's friends are literally in Hebrew 'the men of my peace' (Jer. 20.10, AV familiars; Jer. 38.22, AV friends). Isaiah's condemnation of wicked and unjust men is that they have not known the way of peace. They have been wreckers of personal relationships. Seek peace, says the Psalmist, and pursue it (Ps. 34.14). Do everything to get the relationship with your fellow-men right.

(b) It is the word of the right relationship between nation and nation, as, for instance, when Joshua makes peace with the men of Gibeon (Joshua 9.15).

(c) It is the word of the right relationship between man and God. Between God and his own there is a covenant of peace, which makes it certain that the mountains and the hills will sooner be removed than God's steadfast kindness depart from men (Isa. 54.10). Jeremiah declares that God thinks thoughts of peace towards men (Jer. 29.11).

It is easy to see how great a word peace is. It is far more than a negative state in which trouble has temporarily ceased. It describes health of body, welfare and security, perfect serenity and tranquillity, a life and a state in which a man is perfectly related to his fellow-men and to his God. Truly peace is a word which comes into the NT vocabulary trailing clouds of glory.

In the NT the word *peace, eirēnē,* occurs eighty-eight times, and it occurs in every book. The NT is the book of peace.

The commonest of all its occurrences is in greetings. The normal greeting in an NT letter is, 'Grace to you and peace' (Rom. 1.7; I Cor. 1.3; II Cor. 1.2; Gal. 1.3; Eph. 1.2; Phil. 1.2; Col. 1.2; I Thess. 1.1; II Thess. 1.2; Philemon 3; cp. I Tim. 1.2; II Tim. 1.2; Titus 1.4; I Peter 1.2; II Peter 1.2; II John 3; Rev. 1.4). This is a specially significant greeting. *Grace* is *charis*; and *charis* is the noun from *chairein* which is the normal beginning of a *pagan* letter. It is usually translated, 'Greetings!', and it could mean, as we have seen, 'Joy be with you!'. *Peace* is *eirēnē*, and it is the normal and ordinary greeting in a *Jewish* letter. It is as if the Christian letter writers took and joined together the pagan and the Jewish greetings, as if to say, 'In Jesus Christ all that Jew and Gentile ever dreamed of, and ever wished for themselves and for others has come true. In Jesus Christ for Jew and for Gentile, for Hebrew and for Greek, there is everything for man's highest good.' All blessings are gathered up in the perfect welfare offered in Jesus Christ.

In the NT peace has certain sources from which it comes.

Peace comes from believing. It is Paul's prayer for the Christians at Rome that the God of hope would fill them with all joy and peace in believing (Rom. 15.13). Peace comes from the certainty of the wisdom, the love and the power of God. Peace comes from staking life on the belief that what Jesus said about God is true.

Peace comes from belief which has turned to action. There is glory and honour and peace for everyone who does good, for Jew and for Greek alike (Rom. 2.10). Peace comes from the obedience which is founded on complete trust in God. The Christian life has a foreground of intense activity against a background of wise passivity in which the Christian rests in God.

Peace comes from God. Paul speaks of the peace of God which passes all understanding (Phil. 4.7). In all probability that does not so much mean that the peace of God passes the power of the human mind to comprehend as it means the peace of God passes the ability of the human mind to contrive. Peace is something which God gives far more than it is something which man creates.

Peace is the gift of Jesus Christ. When the Risen Christ returned to his own people, his greeting was, 'Peace be with you' (John 20.19, 21, 26). As Dr James Stewart has put it, when Jesus left men in the flesh he had no material goods or possessions to bequeath to them. Nevertheless Jesus too made his last will and testament: 'Peace I leave with you; my peace I give to you' (John 14.27). In the last analysis peace is not something which a man achieves, but something which a man accepts.

In the NT peace has one meaning more often than any other, and it is a meaning which was carried over from Jewish thought and usage. *Peace is right relationships in every sphere of life.*

(a) Peace is right relationships *within the home.* In I Cor. 7.12-16 Paul deals with a problem which the Corinthian church had raised. There was a party within the Corinthian church which believed that, if one partner in a marriage became a Christian and the other remained a heathen, the Christian partner should leave the heathen partner and so break up and put an end to the marriage. Paul strongly advises against any such course. The duty of the Christian partner is not to leave the heathen partner but to bring the heathen partner to Jesus Christ. And then he gives the reason: 'For God has called us to peace' (I Cor. 7.15). This word peace describes the unbreakable unity of relationship which should exist between husband and wife within the home.

(b) Peace is the new relationship *between Jew and Gentile*. Jesus, says Paul, is our peace, for he has made us both one, and has broken down the dividing wall of hostility. He has created in himself one new man in place of the two, so making peace (Eph. 2.14-17). There is a double picture here. The Temple in Jerusalem consisted of a series of courts of increasing holiness and sacredness. The outermost court was the Court of the Gentiles into which any man of any nation might enter. Then there came the Court of the Women, beyond which women might not go except to make some stipulated sacrifice. Then there came the Court of the Israelites, beyond which no lay person could go. The innermost court was the Court of the Priests, at the end of which there stood the Temple proper and the Holy Place, and where the altars were. Between the Court of the Gentiles and the Court of the Women there was a quite low balustrade called the *chel*; and inset into it at intervals there was an inscription : 'No person of another race is to enter within the balustrade and embankment around the Holy Place. Whoever is caught so doing will be answerable for his own death, which will follow.' Quite literally there was a dividing wall between Jew and Gentile, an absolute separation. That wall was erected by the Jews, but on the Gentile side there was an invisible wall of hatred and suspicion and anti-Semitism which shut the Jew out. With the coming of Jesus the wall of separation was broken down; the racial difference was wiped out. In the Jewish morning prayer there is a thanksgiving in which the male Jew thanks God that God has not made him a Gentile, a slave, or a woman. But it is Paul's great statement that in Christ there is neither Jew or Greek, slave or free, male or female

(Gal. 3.28). In Jesus Christ the barriers are down, and in him alone the right relationship between nation and nation and race and race can be established.

(c) Peace describes the new relationship which must exist *within the Church*. In the Church Christians must maintain the unity of the Spirit in the bond of peace (Eph. 4.3). In Colossians Paul uses a vivid metaphor. 'Let the peace of God,' he says, 'rule in your hearts' (Col. 3.15). The word he uses for *to rule* is a word from the games; it is the word which is used of an umpire giving decisions. Within the Church the peace of God is to be the umpire of all decisions within our hearts. Decisions are not to be governed by personal ambition, the desire for personal prestige, bitterness, the unforgiving spirit; they are to be governed by the peace of God; they are to be made in that personal relationship with men which a relationship to God alone makes possible.

(d) Peace describes the Christian relationship *between man and man*. It is the binding duty of every Christian to strive to create and to maintain that relationship. The Christian must strive for peace with all men (Heb. 12.14). The Christian must labour to be found by Christ in peace, that is, in a right relationship with his fellow-men (II Peter 3.14). The condemnation of evil men is that they have not known the way of peace (Rom. 3.17). There is an implied promise and an implied warning here. No man can do a more Christian work than to establish right relations among men. And God will certainly not hold guiltless the man who is a disturber of personal relationships within the Church. The peacemaker is doing the work of God; the trouble-maker is doing the work of the devil.

(e) Peace describes *the new relationship between man and God*. We have peace with God because through the work of Jesus Christ we have entered into a new relationship with him (Rom. 5.1). Jesus made peace, that is, he established a right relationship, between God and man, through the blood of his cross (Col. 1.20). Through the work of Jesus Christ the fear, the estrangement, the terror, the distance is gone and we are at home with God.

It may well be said that that new relationship is summed up in the new word by which through Jesus we can address

God. Jesus himself called God *Abba* (Mark 14.36), and through the Spirit it is possible for us to use the same word (Rom. 8.15). *Abba* in ancient Palestine, as *yaba* still is among the Arabs today, was the word by which a little child addressed his father in the family circle. Any English translation is grotesque for the meaning is Daddy. What an infinity of difference between that and Manoah's terrified cry to his wife: 'We shall surely die because we have seen God' (Judg. 13.22).

Peace is this completely new relationship which Jesus Christ made possible between man and God.

It is clear that this peace is something of infinite value; and it is clear that its attainment on the human side is no easy task. We have said that this peace is the gift of God, and so it is, for in the NT God is called the God of peace no fewer than six times (Rom. 15.33; 16.20; Phil. 4.9; II Cor. 13.11; I Thess. 5.23; Heb. 13.20, 21). But though all God's greatest gifts are freely given, there is also a sense in which they are not given away. They must be intensely desired and strenuously sought. So the NT uses three great words for man's part in the search for this peace. We must *seek* peace and *pursue* it (I Peter 3.11). We must be *zealous* to be found by him at peace (II Peter 3.14). The word for *to seek* is *zētein*, and it means to make peace the object of all our endeavour. The word for *to pursue* is *diōkein*, which means to hunt down as a hunter might. The word for to be zealous is *spoudazein* which meant *to seek for a thing with a burning enthusiasm*. That peace which is right relationships does not come easily or automatically, but when we desire it with our whole hearts, when we seek it with our whole minds, when we strain every faculty to find it and to maintain it, then God opens his hand and most abundantly gives.

MAKROTHUMIA

Patience Divine and Human

Makrothumia, the noun, *makrothumos*, the adjective, and *makrothumein*, the verb, are in the AV all expressed by the idea of *long-suffering* and *patience*. They are very expressive words. In English we speak of a person having a *short temper*, or of him being *short-tempered*. We do not use what should be the corresponding phrase a *long temper*, nor do we speak about people being *long-tempered*. If we did these words would precisely translate *makrothumos*, for *makros* means *long* and *thumos* means *temper*. We have in English the word *magnanimity*, which means *great heartedness*. In the Vulgate *makrothumia* is translated quite literally by the Latin word *longanimitas*, and the first editions of the Roman Catholic Rheims Bible tried to introduce into the English language the word *longanimity*. In II Peter 3.15 it translates: 'The longanimitie of our Lord count salvation', and in Col. 1.11 it counsels all Christians to walk 'in all patience and longanimitie'. There is no reason why this word should not exist in English, but it never became naturalized, although it would have perfectly expressed the idea in this group of Greek words.

Makrothumia expresses a certain attitude both to people and to events. It expresses the attitude to people which never loses patience with them, however unreasonable they may be, and which never loses hope for them, however unlovely and unteachable they may be. It expresses the attitude to events which never admits defeat, and which never loses its hope and its faith, however dark the situation may be, and however incomprehensible events may be, and however sore the chastening of God may be. It is a quality of which the NT commentators have given many a great definition. Trench says that it describes 'a long holding out of the mind, before it gives room to action or to passion'. T. K. Abbott says that *makrothumia* is 'the self-restraint which does not hastily retaliate a wrong'. Plummer says that it is 'the forbearance which endures injuries and evil deeds without being provoked to anger or revenge'. Moffatt describes it as 'the tenacity with which faith holds out'. In the *Testament of Joseph* (2.7) there is the phrase, '*Makrothumia* is a great medicine'. There is a saying of Menander which Plutarch quotes: 'Since you are a man, never ask from the gods for a life without trouble, but ask for *makrothumia*.' We might well translate *makrothumia* 'the power to see things through'.

Makrothumia is not a word of classical Greek, yet it came into the Christian vocabulary with a great history, for it is one of the great words of the Greek OT. In the OT it moves in three spheres.

(a) It means *patience with events*. The most illuminating use of the word in this sense is in I Macc. 8.4. There the writer attributes the greatness of Rome to her policy and her patience, to her *makrothumia*, and, as R. C. Trench says, that *makrothumia* was expressed in Rome's determination 'never to make peace under defeat'. The Romans had that staying power which might lose a battle, and which might even lose a campaign, but which would never admit defeat in a war. It is said that the test of an army is how it fights when its soldiers are hungry and tired. *Makrothumia* is the spirit which will neither recognize nor admit defeat.

(b) It means *patience with people*. It means the spirit which never loses patience with people or hope for people, which will never turn to bitterness, and which will never agree to be ultimately repulsed. In this spirit and this quality the OT sees the source of the greatest things in life.

i. It is the basis of *forgiveness*. It is the spirit which makes a man defer his anger (Prov. 19.11), and to refuse to be angry is to be halfway to forgiving.

ii. It is the basis of *humility*. The patient in spirit is better than the proud in spirit (Eccles. 7.8). *Makrothumia* prevents a man from putting himself in the centre of the picture and from making his feelings the criterion of everything.

iii. It is obviously the foundation of *fellowship*. A hot-tempered man stirs up strife, but the man who is slow to anger quiets contention (Prov. 15.18). The man whose tem-

per is on a hair-trigger destroys friendship and fellowship;
the man whose temper is under control cements fellowship,
and refuses to allow strife to arise.

iv. It is the basis of *all good personal relationships*. As
Moffatt translates Prov. 25.15, 'An angry man is pacified by
forbearance.' *Makrothumia* always soothes and never exa-
cerbates. It refuses to allow a breach in personal relationships, and it goes far to heal a breach when a breach has
arisen.

v. It is the basis of all *true wisdom*. The man who is
slow to wrath is of great understanding, but he that is
hasty of spirit exalts folly (Prov. 14.29). The Jewish saying
has it: 'An irritable man cannot teach,' and equally an
irritable man cannot learn. The first necessity of learning is
patience.

vi. It is the basis of *lasting joy*. As Ben Sirach has it, 'A
furious man cannot be justified, for the sway of his fury
shall be his destruction. But a patient man will bear for a
time, and afterwards joy will come to him' (Ecclus 1.22).
The hasty man destroys his own happiness and the happiness of others; the man of the serene temper brings happiness to himself and to all with whom he comes into contact.

vii. It is the basis of *all true power*. He that is slow to
anger is better than the mighty; and he that ruleth his
spirit than he that taketh a city (Prov. 16.32). The man who
can rule himself is the man who can rule others.

(c) But the greatest fact about this word is that it describes the character of God himself.

There is a description of God which runs like a refrain
through the OT. God passed before Moses and proclaimed:
'The Lord, the Lord, a God merciful and gracious, *slow to
anger* and abounding in steadfast love and faithfulness' (Ex.
34.6). 'Thou art a God,' says Nehemiah, 'ready to forgive,
gracious and merciful, slow to anger, and abounding in
steadfast love' (Neh. 9.17). Again and again in the Psalms
we find the great rejoicing refrain: 'The Lord is merciful
and gracious, slow to anger and abounding in steadfast
love' (Pss. 103.8; 86.15; 145.8). It was precisely this that
Jonah did not realize and had to learn (Jonah 4.2). It is in

this long-suffering, this slowness to anger, of God that we see certain great truths about the attitude of God to the sinner.

i. The *makrothumia* of God is *the sinner's hope*. It is because God is gracious and merciful, slow to anger, and abounding in steadfast love that Joel urges the people to rend their hearts and not their garments and to return to God (Joel 2.13). Without God's patience there could be no place left for repentance.

ii. The *makrothumia* of God is *the sinner's warning*. The sinner dare not think that, even if nothing has happened, he has escaped the consequences of his sin. 'Say not, I have sinned, and what harm has happened to me? For the Lord is long-suffering. He will in nowise let thee go' (Ecclus 5.4). It is indeed in his long-suffering that God visits the sins of the fathers on the children to the third and fourth generation (Num. 14.18). It is because God is patient that God has the last word.

iii. The *makrothumia* of God can be the sinner's *doom*. In II Macc. 6.14 there is the terrible thought that God is patient with men, and leaves them to themselves so that they may come to the height of their sin—and then the judgment comes. A man may use the patience of God for his own destruction.

We now turn to the use and the meaning of *makrothumia* in the NT. In the NT it moves in the same three spheres of meaning as it does in the OT.

(a) *Makrothumia* speaks of the patience of God.

i. It is in II Peter that the patience of God is presented at its widest. 'Count the forbearance of the Lord as salvation' (II Peter 3.15). It is a matter of doubt as to whether 'the Lord' is Jesus or God, but the sense of the saying is not really affected. The background against which II Peter is written is the background of a disappointment and disillusionment at the slowness of the Second Coming of Jesus Christ. And the writer's point is that this slowness is not dilatoriness; it is patience. It is the opportunity for men to repent and to believe the gospel, to turn their sinfulness into holiness, to make their unpreparedness prepared. Behind it there is the thought that God would have been quite justified in blasting the world out of existence, that, if he had been a man, he would long since have done so, but in his patience he waits to give men the opportunity to accept salvation.

Exactly the same thought, and even more personally, is in Paul. In I Tim. 1.12-16—surely a genuine Pauline fragment even if the Pastorals are not Pauline as a whole as they stand—Paul tells how he blasphemed, persecuted, insulted Christ, how he was nothing less than the chief of sinners. But in him Jesus displayed his perfect patience. Patiently Jesus waited until Paul the persecutor became Paul ready to be the apostle.

The patience of God waits when the impatience of man would long since have acted in destructive anger.

ii. But God's patience is more than simple waiting; God's patience is calling men to repent. God is forbearing, because he does not wish that any should perish, but that all should reach repentance (II Peter 3.9). Men must never presume on the kindness and the forbearance of God, for that kindness is not meant to be an opportunity to sin, but is rather an invitation to repentance (Rom. 2.4). God does not only wait for men to come home to him; in Jesus Christ he came to seek them and to save them; and still even yet he woos them with the promptings and the pleadings of his Holy Spirit.

iii. As in the thought of the OT, that very patience of God may be used by man for his own destruction. God's patience with Israel can be read in the light of allowing the wayward nation to go its own way until its final rejection had to happen (Rom. 9.22).

God waits in patience; God seeks in patience; and that waiting and seeking are meant to be for man's salvation, but man in his folly can turn them into condemnation.

(b) The NT speaks of *makrothumia* in relation to our fellow-men.

i. *Makrothumia* is nothing less than the badge and the uniform of the Christian life. The Christian must walk with all lowliness, meekness and patience, forbearing one another in love (Eph. 4.2). The Christian must put on as a garment compassion, kindness, lowliness, meekness, patience, forbearing one another (Col. 3.12). Forbearance and kindness are just as much the mark of the Christian life as any of the martyr virtues (II Cor. 6.6). Christian love must suffer long; it must be patient and kind (I Cor. 13.4). However unsatisfactory men may be, the Christian must be patient with them all (I Thess. 5.14). The man of the world may lose his temper and his patience and his belief in men; the Christian can never do so.

ii. It is not without significance that *makrothumia* occupies a high place among the Christian virtues in the Pastoral Epistles. The patient love of the Christian teacher is contrasted with the folly of the false teachers (II Tim. 3.10). The young missionary is instructed to be 'unfailing in patience' (II Tim. 4.2). And no doubt there the word combines both its senses, for the teacher and the preacher must never lose faith in men, however unresponsive they may seem to be, and must never allow himself to despair, however hostile circumstances are. No man can preach or teach without *makrothumia*.

(c) *Makrothumia* describes the response of the Christian towards circumstances and events. Paul prays that the Colossians may have endurance and patience with joy (Col. 1.11). The Christian patience is not a grim, bleak acceptance of a situation; even the patience is irradiated with joy. The Christian waits, not as one who waits for the night, but as one who waits for the morning. This unwearied patience is as much a part of the Christian life as the martyr virtues (II Cor. 6.6). It was because Abraham patiently endured that he received the promise, and it must be so with the Christian who has a like faith (Heb. 6.12-15).

It may be that the hardest lesson of all to learn is how to wait, how to wait when nothing seems to be happening, and when all the circumstances seem calculated to bring nothing but discouragement. James insists that the Christian must be like the prophets who again and again had to wait for the action of God; he must be like the farmer who sows the seed and who then throughout the slow months waits until the harvest comes (James 5.7-10). It may well be that this is the hardest task of all for an age which has made a god of speed.

In some ways *makrothumia* is the greatest virtue of all. It is not clad with romance and glamour; it has not the excitement of sudden adventurous action; but it is the very virtue of God himself. God in his *makrothumia* bears with the sins, the refusals and the rebellions of men. God in his *makrothumia* refuses to abandon hope of the world which he created and which so often turns its back on its Creator. And man in his life on earth must reproduce God's undefeatable patience with people and God's undiscourageable patience with events.

CHRĒSTOTĒS

The Divine Kindness

The fifth virtue in the fruit of the Spirit is *chrēstotēs*. Here in Galatians the AV translates it *gentleness*; but the regular translation of it in the AV where it occurs elsewhere is *kindness* (II Cor. 6.6; Eph. 2.7; Col. 3.12; Titus 3.4). *Kindness* is the translation of the RV, the RSV, and Kingsley Williams, while Moffatt translates it *kindliness*.

R. C. Trench says of *chrēstotēs* that 'it is a beautiful word for the expression of a beautiful grace'. The Vulgate very beautifully translates the word either by *bonitas*, which is *goodness* or *bounty*, or by *benignitas*, whence comes the adjective *benign*. The Roman Catholic Rheims translation comes very near the meaning when here it translates *chrēstotēs* by *benignity* and in II Cor. 6.6 by *sweetness*. Plummer on II Cor. 6.6 says that *chrēstotēs* in men is 'the sympathetic kindliness or sweetness of temper which puts others at their ease, and shrinks from giving pain'.

It is a word which came into Christian vocabulary with a great history. Marcus Aurelius uses it to describe God. He speaks of the kindness with which God has glorified man (*Meditations* 8.34). He talks of man's duty to forgive the sinner and the foolish man, and that duty is a duty because the gods are *chrēstoi*, they are kind, for they too

D

forgive the sinner (*Meditations* 8.11). The pagan philoso
phers sang the praises of the virtue of kindness. Marcus
Aurelius lays it down that 'kindness (*to eumenes*) is irresis-
tible, when it is sincere and no mock smile or a mask
assumed' (*Meditations* 11.18). Epictetus says that a man has
lost the very essence of manhood, the distinguishing quality
which makes him a man, when he has lost his kindness (*to
eugnōmon*) and his fidelity. He says that we know a coin
and we know to whom a coin belongs by the imprint on it;
and then he says that we know that a man belongs to God
when he has on him the imprint of gentleness, generosity,
patience and affection, when he is *hēmeros, koinōnikos,
anektikos, philallēlos.*

Even the heathen philosophers would have laid it down
that it is in kindness which makes a man kin to God.

But it is in the LXX that *chrēstotēs* finds its greatest
background for NT thought. In the LXX *chrēstos*
and *chrēstotēs* are used more commonly of God than
of anyone else. It is something of a joyous revelation
to discover that, when the AV calls God *good*, again and
again the meaning is not moral goodness but kindness.
Again and again, when we go back to the LXX, we
find that *good* is *chrēstos* and goodness is *chrēstotēs*. Again
and again the Psalmist sings: 'Give thanks to God for he is
kind, for his steadfast love lasts for ever' (Pss. 106.1; 107.1;
136.1; Jer. 40.11). What moves the heart of the Psalmist is
not the moral goodness of God, but the sheer kindness
of God. His only claim to God's gifts, and his only hope
of forgiveness lie in the fact that God is kind; his only
prayer is that God should hear him because God is kind,
and that God should be merciful to him because God is
kind (Pss. 69.16; 86.3; 100.5; 109.21). 'Remember me,' he
prays, 'according to thy steadfast love, for thy kindness' sake, O Lord' (Ps. 25.7). 'God is the only and the
kindly (gracious) king' (II Macc. 1.24). The priests and
Levites sing their anthem of praise to God because his
kindness (mercy) and glory are for ever in all Israel (I Esd.
5.61).

The goodness of God is not a moral holiness from which
a man might shrink in fear; it is a kindness which draws

men to him with cords of love. The OT sees this kindness of God expressed in certain ways.

i. The kindness of God is expressed *in nature*. 'The Lord will give kindness,' says the Psalmist, 'and our land shall yield her fruit' (Ps. 85.12). God will bless the crown of the year because of his kindness (Ps. 64.11). When God opens his hand, men are satisfied with kindness (Ps. 104.28). The bounty of nature is the expression of the kindness of God.

ii. The kindness of God is expressed in *the events of history*. The Psalmist will utter the memory of God's kindness (Ps. 145.7). He gives thanks to God for what God has done; God's name is good, kind, before the saints (Ps. 52.9). God has gone before the king with blessings of kindness and has put a crown upon his head (Ps. 20.3).

iii. The kindness of God is expressed even in *the judgments of God*. The Psalmist prays that God will take away the reproach that he feared, for his judgments are kind (Ps. 119.39). If God's judgments were simply morally good, then there would be nothing left but fear; but God's judgments are kind and therein lies our hope.

iv. The kindness of God is expressed in *the instruction of God*. 'Thou art kind,' says the Psalmist to God, 'therefore, in thy kindness teach me thy ordinances' (Ps. 119.65-68). God is upright and kind, and for that very reason, he will instruct sinners in the way (Ps. 25.8). God's kindness is expressed in the revelation of his will and his holiness to men.

v. The kindness of God comes very specially to certain people. It comes to those who are *afflicted*. The Lord is kind to those who wait on him in the day of their affliction (Nahum 1.7). It comes to those who are *poor*, to those who know too well their own helplessness and inadequacy. God in his kindness has prepared for the poor (Ps. 67.10). It comes to those who *hope* and *trust* in God. It is the appeal of the Psalmist that men should taste and see that God is kind, and that joy comes to the man who places his hope in him (Ps. 34.8). It comes to those who *reverence* and *fear* him. There is an abundant multitude of kindnesses laid up for those who fear God (Ps. 30.19). It comes to those who *wait* on God. The Lord is kind to those who wait on him (Ps. 145.9).

vi. It therefore comes as no surprise that it is the possession of this kindness which makes a man a good man, and the neglect of it which brings the condemnation of God. It is the lament of the Psalmist that there is none who does good, that there is none that is kind, not even one (Ps. 52.3). Hope in the Lord, says the Psalmist, and do good. Hope in the Lord, and be kind (Ps. 36.3). It is the tragedy of life that there is none who does goodness, that there is none who is kind (Ps. 13.1, 3). The good man, the kind man, is the man who pities and lends (Ps. 112.5). Caring is the very essence of the good life; to be good is to be kind, and to be kind is to be good.

vii. Finally, in regard to the OT, we may note that the word *chrēstos* can describe something which is very precious, for in Ezekiel it is twice used to describe precious stones (Ezek. 27.22; 28.13); and that it can describe something which is good and useful, for in Jeremiah it is used to describe good figs in contrast to fruit that is rotten (Jer. 24.2, 4, 5). This does add something to the meaning of the word, for there can be a kindness which is weakening and enervating, but the kindness which the OT demands from men and constantly attributes to God is profitable and precious and health-giving.

We now turn to the way in which these words are used in the NT.

i. The NT too speaks of the kindness and the forbearance of God (Rom. 2.4), and Paul has nothing but condemnation for the man who does not see that this kindness of God is designed to lead us to repentance (Rom. 2.4). It should in fact be that very kindness of God which is the dynamic of Christian goodness. It is because men have tasted that the Lord is kind that they should lay all sinful things aside (I Peter 2.3). The kindness of God must never be regarded as providing an opportunity to sin; it is a terrible thing to seek to try to trade on the kindness of God. In any event, this kindness of God is not an easy-going sentimental thing, because hand in hand with it goes the severity of God (Rom. 11.22). In God there is strength and gentleness combined.

The kindness of God is a universal thing, for God is kind even to the unthankful and to the evil (Luke 6.35). The fact is that it is impossible to live in the world and to enjoy the light of the sun without experiencing the kindness of God; there is no man who is not indebted to this kindness for it is universally bestowed, not according to man's deserving, but according to God's graciousness in giving.

In this kindness of God there is a saving power. It is the kindness of God our Saviour (Titus 3.4). It is a kindness which forgives past sin and which by the Holy Spirit strengthens men for future goodness. It not only forgives the sinner; it changes the sinner into a good man. And that is why the kindness of God to us is above all exemplified and demonstrated in Jesus Christ (Eph. 2.7). The coming of Jesus Christ is God's supreme act of kindness, and in Jesus Christ the kindness of God is enmanned and incarnated.

ii. Just as in the OT so in the NT this kindness is the characteristic of the good life. Paul quotes the Psalmist that the tragedy of life is that there is none who does good, there is none who is kind (Rom. 3.12). The danger of life is that bad company corrupts the good morals which a Christian should always show (I Cor. 15.33). This kindness is one of the things which a Christian must put on as part of the uniform of the Christian life (Col. 3.12).

It is in this kindness that Christians must forgive one another, and that forgiveness is patterned on nothing other and nothing less than God's forgiveness of ourselves. 'Be kind to one another, tender-hearted, forgiving one another, as God in Christ forgave you' (Eph. 4.32). Even the sterner virtues lose their value if this kindness is not present in life (II Cor. 6.6).

There remain two instances of this word in the NT, and they have something still to add to the picture in this word. In Luke 5.29 *chrēstos* is used of wine which has grown old and mellow. The harshness and the roughness and the bitterness are banished by Christian kindness and the mellow graciousness of Christian love remains. In Matt. 11.30 Jesus says: 'My yoke is easy.' There *chrēstos* can mean *well-fitting*. The service of Christ is not tyrannically imposed upon a man; it does not act like a slave-driver; it is a kindly thing, and the task Christ gives a man is tailor-made for him.

This Christian kindness is a lovely thing, and its loveliness comes from the fact that Christian kindness means treating others in the way in which God has treated us.

AGATHŌSUNĒ

The Generous Goodness

The difficulty with the sixth virtue in the fruit of the Spirit is to define more exactly what it means. All the other eight virtues and graces are quite definite adornments of the Christian character; but in English *goodness* is a wide and a general term. The difficulty about the word *goodness* is that it takes its meaning from its context, and from the sphere in which the particular excellence described lies. We may, for instance, say: 'That is a good animal.' If the animal is reared for killing and eating, the goodness will consist in the massive flesh and fat on it. If the animal is kept for breeding, the goodness will lie in its pedigree. If the animal is intended for racing, the goodness will lie in its trained muscles and in the fact that it has no superfluous flesh on it. Usually we say that a man is good *at something*; we define the sphere in which the goodness operates. A man might be good at languages and bad at mathematics; he might be good at games and bad at academic studies; he might be good at his work and yet bad as a husband and a father. He might be good in character but bad in health. Goodness itself is a quite general term, and we must clearly try to define more closely the sphere in which Paul is using this word. We shall begin by quoting two suggestions as to the general line of the meaning of goodness. The word itself is *agathōsunē*.

The two interpretations we quote link *chrēstotēs* and *agathōsunē* very closely together. Lightfoot distinguished the two by saying that there is more activity in *agatho-*

sunē. Chrēstotēs is a quality of heart and emotion; *agathō-sunē* is a quality of conduct and action. He writes : '*Chrēs-totēs* is potential *agathōsunē, agathōsunē* is energizing *chrēstotēs.*' On this basis we might say that *agathōsunē* is *chrēstotēs* in action. It is an attractive idea, but in point of fact there is no actual evidence that the words are so distinguished in use.

R. C. Trench follows the interpretation of Jerome. According to this interpretation there is a quality of gracious and attractive kindness in *chrēstotēs* whereas in *agathōsunē* there can be much more sternness and austerity than in *chrēstotēs. In chrēstotēs* it is the kindness which is stressed; in *agathōsunē* it is the moral judgment which is stressed. So Trench says that *agathōsunē* may well be displayed in zeal for goodness and truth, in rebuking, correcting and chastening. It was *agathōsunē* that Jesus showed when he drove the buyers and sellers out of the Temple (Matt. 21.13), and when he uttered his threats and condemnations against the Scribes and Pharisees (Matt. 23); but it was *chrēstotēs* he showed when he dealt gently with the penitence in the heart of the woman who was a sinner and who anointed his feet (Luke 7.37-50).

The difficulty of defining the meaning of *agathōsunē* is accentuated by the fact that it is not a common word. It does not occur in secular Greek at all. In the LXX it occurs about thirteen times; and in the NT there are only three other occurrences of the word.

We might have tried to define the meaning of this noun by examining the meaning of the corresponding adjective *agathos,* but here we meet the opposite difficulty. *Agathos* is one of the commonest words in Greek. In the LXX it occurs almost 520 times and in the NT 100 times; and its range is very wide. It can describe a tree (Matt. 7.17); a gift (Matt. 7.11); a man (Matt. 12.35); a slave (Matt. 25.21); a teacher, in this case, Jesus himself (Mark 10.17); fertile ground (Luke 8.8); a man's conscience (Acts 23.1); the will of God (Rom. 12.2); the Christian hope (II Thess. 2.16); fruits and crops (James 3.17); words and deeds (Eph. 2.10; II Thess. 2.17). The word *agathos* is so wide in meaning that it can and does describe that which is excellent in any sphere. Unless we can go on to concentrate its meaning a little more, it will not help us to define the meaning of *agathōsunē* here. Let us, then, examine such material as we have. Let us look at the word in the LXX.

i. In the LXX *agathōsunē can mean goodness in general.* The Psalmist writes: 'Thou hast loved wickedness more than goodness', and the parallel is, 'Unrighteousness better than to speak righteousness' (Ps. 52.3). There *agathōsunē* is simply a wide general term for goodness as opposed to wickedness.

ii. In the LXX it can mean *prosperity in life.* 'In the day of *prosperity*,' says the Preacher, 'live joyfully' (Eccles. 7.15). There is no use in a successful life if a man gets no joy of his prosperity (Eccles. 6.3). With his deep pessimism the Preacher says that even if a man has lived for two thousand years yet he has been no *good* (Eccles. 6.6). 'It is a fine thing,' he says, 'for a man to eat and to drink, and to enjoy the *good* of all his labour' (Eccles. 5.17). Wisdom is better than weapons of war, but a reckless sinner can destroy much good, that is, he can undo much prosperity (Eccles. 9.18). Eccles. 5.10(11) is an obscure verse. The LXX has it: 'In the multitude of good they are increased that eat it.' The AV has, 'When *goods* are increased, they are increased that eat them.' Moffatt best brings out the meaning, 'The more a man gains, the more there are to spend it.' Certainly in the LXX *agathōsunē* means *prosperity*, but that does not greatly help us here.

iii. In the LXX it can have the idea of *benefit.* 'For whom do I labour,' says the Preacher, 'and deprive my soul of good?' (Eccles. 4.8). The idea is, Why do I deprive myself of the benefits I might enjoy? The last words of the book of Nehemiah are: 'Remember me, O our God, for good' (Neh. 13.31). This again is a meaning which does not help us very much.

iv. In the LXX it can have the idea of *generosity*. It is Nehemiah's charge against the people: 'They have not served thee in the kingdom, and in thy great *goodness* which thou gavest to them' (Neh. 9.35). He says of the people who entered into the Promised Land: 'So they ate, and were filled, and grew fat, and delighted in thy great goodness' (Neh. 9.25). They revelled, as we might say, in the generosity of God. *Agathōsunē*, then, has the idea of generosity, particularly the generosity of God.

The NT evidence for this word is very meagre. We can only set down the three instances in which it occurs other than in this passage. In II Thess. 2.17 Paul prays for his people that God may for them fulfil every *good resolve*. In Eph. 5.9 Paul says that the fruit of the Spirit is all *goodness*, and righteousness, and truth. In Rom. 15.14 Paul writes of the Roman Christians: 'I myself also am persuaded of you, my brethren, that ye also are full of *goodness*, filled with all knowledge, able also to admonish one another.'

We have still very little help to pinpoint the meaning of this word.

We shall best come to the meaning of this word by comparing it with two other words, with one of which it is closely parallel, and to the other of which it is antithetic.

The word *agathos* quite often goes with the word *dikaios*, and the word *agathōsunē* is often connected with the word *dikaiosunē*. *Dikaios* means *just* and *kikaiosunē* means *justice*. The Greeks defined the just man as the man who gives to gods and to men what is their due. The Greek writers on this very basis define and compare and contrast *dikaiosunē* and *agathōsunē*. *Justice*, they say, is the quality which gives a man what is due to him; *goodness* is the quality which is out to do far more than that, and which desires to give a man all that is to his benefit and his help. The man who is *just* sticks to the letter of his bond; the man who is *good* goes far beyond it.

There is an interesting application of this. The Gnostics said that the God of the OT is *dikaios*, *just*, while the God of the NT is *agathos*, *generous* and *kind*. Broadly speaking, in the OT the picture is of a God who set the moral law in operation, and from whom every man receives according to his deserts. Broadly speaking, in the NT the picture is of a God who deals with men, not by law, but by grace, and who gives them, not what they deserve, but what his love freely and undeservedly gives. The *Clementine Homilies* say that God is both *agathos* and *dikaios*, *agathos* in that he forgives the penitent sinner, *dikaios* in that every man receives according to his deeds after he has repented. The great characteristic of *dikaiosunē* is the accurate payment to a man of the reward or punishment his deeds merit. The great characteristic of *agathōsunē* is the generosity which gives a man what he never could have earned. This is to say that the primary idea of *agathōsunē* is generosity.

In justice there is no real room for pity and mercy, for pity and mercy would do no more than interfere with the course of abstract justice. In goodness pity and mercy are integral parts, for goodness is the generosity which is undeserved.

The word which is opposite in meaning to *agathos* is *ponēros*. *Ponēros* is a quite general word for *evil* or *bad*. God makes his sun to shine on the evil (*ponēros*) and on the good (*agathos*) (Matt. 5.45). Men acquired the knowledge of good and *evil* (Gen. 2.9, 17). *Ho Ponēros*, the Evil One, is one of the commonest titles of Satan (Matt. 6.13; Eph. 6.16; I John 2.14).

But *ponēros* has one special usage. This usage comes out particularly in the Parable of the Labourers in the Vineyard. At the end of the day all the labourers were paid the same, and those who had worked the longer hours complained. The master of the vineyard answered: 'Is it not lawful for me to do what I like with mine own? Is thine eye evil (*ponēros*) because I am good (*agathos*)?' (Matt. 20.15). Moffatt translates: 'Have you a grudge because I am generous?' The RSV translates: 'Do you begrudge my generosity?' Quite clearly in that passage *ponēros* means *mean, niggardly, grudging,* and *agathos* means *liberal, generous.*

It is possible that *ponēros* has the same meaning in two other NT passages. In Matt. 6.23 Jesus says: 'If thine eye be *evil* (*ponēros*) thy whole body shall be full of darkness', which may well mean, 'If you are mean and grudging, niggardly and ungenerous, then your whole life is shadowed and darkened.' In Mark 7.22 Jesus lists among the sins of the spirit *an evil eye*, and once again this can mean a mean, jealous, ungenerous eye.

In the LXX there are certain quite undoubted cases of *ponēros* in this sense. 'Do not eat the bread,' says the Sage, 'of a man who is *stingy* (*ponēros*)' (Prov. 23.6). 'A *miserly* (*ponēros*) man hastens after wealth' (Prov. 28.22).

There are two clear examples of this usage in Deuteronomy. A man who is tender and delicately bred has *an evil eye* (*ponēros*) to his wife and his children and his friends, that is, in his desire for luxury he grudges everything he has to give them (Deut. 28.54). According to the Deuteronomic regulations, in the Year of Release, every seventh year, all debts were cancelled, and a clean sheet was made. In such circumstances it was very natural and indeed prudent for the mean man to refuse to lend anything when the Year of Release was near, in case he never got his money back again, when debts were cancelled. It is therefore laid down that a man must not have an evil eye (*ponēros*) against his poor brother and so give him nothing. That is to say a man must not be so mean that he will not risk lending to the poor at such a time (Deut. 15.9).

Quite clearly *ponēros* often means *mean, niggardly, miserly,* and, therefore, *agathos* will mean *generous, liberal, open-handed.* Here is our clue. The man who is *agathos* is not like the man who is *dikaios* who gives to a man what he has earned, neither less nor more; he is generous to give what was never deserved. The man who is *agathos* is not like the man who is *ponēros* who grudges everything he has to give; he is generous and open-handed and open-hearted. *Agathōsunē* is the generosity which springs from the heart that is kind.

PISTIS

The Virtue of Reliability

The seventh of the graces in the fruit of the Spirit is *pistis,* which the AV translates *faith. Pistis* is one of the commonest words in the NT, for faith is that on which the whole Christian religion is based. But in this list of the fruit of the Spirit *faith* is a misleading translation. In by far the greater number of the occasions on which *pistis* occurs in the NT it means the faith which is absolute trust, absolute self-surrender, absolute confidence, absolute obedience in regard to Jesus Christ. This is what might be called a theological virtue; it is rather the basis of belief and the basis of our whole relationship to God through Jesus Christ. But the virtues listed in the fruit of the Spirit are not *theological* virtues; they are *ethical* virtues : they have to do not so much with our relationship to God as with our relationship to our fellow-men. What *pistis* here means is not *faith* but *faithfulness*; it is the quality of reliability, trustworthiness, which makes a man a person on whom we can utterly rely and whose word we can utterly accept. This is in fact shown by the new translations. The RV and the RSV both have *faithfulness*; Moffatt and Phillips have *fidelity*; C. Kingsley Williams has *honesty*. When we do examine the uses of *pistis* in the NT in this sense, it will often appear that the best translation of all is simply *loyalty*.

The number of times when *pistis* has this sense in the NT are comparatively few. In Matt. 23.23 Jesus charges the Scribes and Pharisees with being meticulous about tithing mint and dill and cummin, and with yet neglecting the weightier matters of the law, justice, mercy and *faith*. The meaning is that they carefully carry out the ritual and ceremonial demands of the law, but they neglect the basic human qualities of justice, kindness and loyalty. Moffatt and Kingsley Williams both have *faithfulness* here. In Titus 2.10 it is laid down that servants must never pilfer, but must show good *fidelity*. A Christian servant must be honest and trustworthy. In Rom. 3.3 Paul compares the fickleness of men with the faithfulness of God. God's promises remain true in spite of all the faithlessness of men. Man's faithlessness can never cancel the faithfulness of God.

It is likely that it is in this sense that the word *pistis* is more than once used in the Revelation. The Revelation is written against a background of persecution, against a situation in which the martyr virtues are the supreme virtues of the Christian, a situation in which the greatest virtue of all is inflexible loyalty to Jesus Christ. The Risen Christ knows that the Christians of Pergamum have to live where Satan's seat is, and he congratulates them that, even in the days when persecution raged, they did not deny their faith in him, that even then their loyalty stood the test (Rev. 2.13). A killing time is a call for the endurance and the faith, that is, the loyalty, of the saints (Rev. 13.10; 14.12).

These are the main NT uses of this word *pistis* in this sense of *fidelity* or *loyalty*; but we do possess a means of developing and amplifying the meaning of the word. The corresponding adjective *pistos* is commoner than the noun. It too has two senses corresponding to the two meanings of *pistis*; it means *believing*, and it means *reliable, dependable, trustworthy, faithful*. Let us then examine its use in this second sense, and we shall see wherein this NT loyalty lies.

i. *Pistos* is characteristically the adjective by which the good and loyal servant is described. It is the prerequisite of a steward that he should be *faithful* (I Cor. 4.2). This is the word which Jesus uses of the trusty and wise servant who is made steward over all the house (Matt. 24.45; Luke 12.42). It is the word of commendation to the good and *faithful* servants in the twin parables of the talents and of the pounds (Matt. 25.21, 23; Luke 19.17). It occurs in the three lessons which are appended to the parable of the unjust steward. He who is *faithful* in little is *faithful* in much. If a man is not *faithful* in the wealth of time, who will give him the wealth of eternity? The trustworthy man is *faithful* with another's goods (Luke 16.10-12). Trustworthiness is the quality for which men look in their fellow-men, and trustworthiness is the quality for which Jesus Christ looks in his followers also.

ii. It is therefore only to be expected that this word should describe the good servant of the gospel, of the Church, and of Jesus Christ. Paul uses it of himself. He thanks Jesus Christ for regarding him as *faithful* and for putting him into the ministry (I Tim. 1.12). The teachings of the Church are to be committed to faithful men who will teach them to others (II Tim. 2.2). Here the word may well have a double sense, and may mean men who are both believing and trustworthy.

Again and again Paul characterizes his helpers as faithful in the Lord. Timothy, Tychicus, Epaphras, Onesimus are so described (I Cor. 4.17; Eph. 6.21; Col. 1.7; 4.9); Peter uses the same word of Silvanus (I Peter 5.12), and John of Gaius (III John 5). The most valuable asset that any leader can possess is those who are faithful and loyal, men on whom he can utterly depend for loyalty and for faithful work.

Not only is *pistos* the word of the Church and its virtues, it is also the word of the domestic virtue, for wives are to be sober and faithful in all things (I Tim. 3.11).

No church and no marriage can stand unless they are based on loyalty.

iii. Especially in the Pastoral Epistles a characteristic usage of *pistos* is in connection with *logos*, which is a *word* or *statement*. A *pistos logos* is a statement on the truth of which the hearer can absolutely rely, and of which he can be quite sure. That Christ Jesus came into the world to save sinners (I Tim. 1.15); that to desire the office of a bishop is to desire a good work (I Tim. 3.1); that the service of God must bring its own suffering (I Tim. 4.9); that those who claim to believe in God must produce good works (Titus 3.8); that the Christian must hold fast to the word on which he can rely (Titus 1.9)—each one of these statements is described as a *pistos logos*, a statement on which there can be no doubt. So in the Revelation the message of the Risen Christ is *faithful* and true (Rev. 21.5; 22.6). A *pistos logos* is a word the truth of which it is impossible to doubt.

iv. *Pistos* describes the man whose loyalty will enable him to die for Jesus Christ. Antipas is the *faithful* martyr of Christ; and the Christian is bidden to be faithful unto death (Rev. 2.10; 3.14). The man who is *pistos* would rather lose his life than his honour.

v. We have not yet reached the full height of this word *pistos*. *Pistos* is more than once used to describe Jesus Christ himself. Jesus is the *faithful* witness, the *faithful* and the true (Rev. 1.5; 19.11). A man may stake his life on the truth of that which Jesus said and came to say. Jesus is the merciful and *faithful* High Priest (Heb. 2.17). A man may utterly depend on him to open the way to God. Jesus is *faithful* to God who appointed him to his task (Heb. 3.2, 5). If we may dare to put it so, not man only, but God also can depend on Jesus. To call a man *pistos* is to call him by nothing less than the title of Jesus himself.

vi. We may take the last and final step beyond which no word can ever go. Again and again *pistos* is a description of God. This is specially so in Paul's letters. The God who called us into the fellowship of his Son is faithful (I Cor. 1.9). God is faithful not to allow us to be tried above what we can bear (I Cor. 10.13). Paul takes his oath that God is true (II Cor. 1.19). The God who called us is faithful and will fulfil his promise and his work (I Thess. 5.24). The God who will establish us and who will keep us from all evil is faithful (II Thess. 3.3). Even if men disbelieve, God remains faithful (II Thess. 2.13). It is as if there runs through the letters of Paul the ever-recurring refrain: 'You can depend on God.'

The writer to the Hebrews insists that we can depend on the God who gave us his promise (Heb. 10.23). Sara in her old age had a child because she believed that she could utterly rely on the promise of God (Heb. 11.11). Peter urges his people even in their sufferings to entrust their souls to the Creator on whom they can depend (I Peter 4.19). If we confess our sin, says John, we can depend on God to forgive (I John 1.9).

With one voice the NT writers witness to that which they themselves had over and over again experienced—the great truth that we can depend on God

Pistos is indeed a great word. It describes the man on whose faithful service we may rely, on whose loyalty we may depend, whose word we can unreservedly accept. It describes the man in whom there is the unswerving and inflexible fidelity of Jesus Christ, and the utter dependability of God.

PRAUTĒS

Strength and Gentleness

The eighth of the graces in the fruit of the Spirit is *prautēs*, which the AV translates meekness. In modern thought and language meekness is not an admirable quality. The word has in it nowadays a suggestion of spinelessness and spiritlessness, and a lack of strength and virility. The only real alternative which the modern translations offer is gentleness, which is better, but which is by no means a perfect translation. As we study this word we shall come to see that there is no one word in English which adequately translates it, and we shall also come to see that it is a word which describes a quality without which a man can never rise to the heights of either the devotional or the practical life.

Prautēs, the *noun*, *praus*, the adjective, and *praunein*, the verb are words on the meaning of which secular Greek throws much light. In secular Greek they are used with a very definite atmosphere and flavour.

i. They are used of persons or things which have in them a certain soothing quality. They are used of words which will soothe a man when he is in a state of anger, bitterness and resentment against life. They are used of an ointment which can soothe the pain of an ulcerous wound. They are used of the gentleness which comes into the tone of the voice of a lover. Once in *The Laws* Plato uses them of a child asking a doctor to treat him in the gentlest possible way. The words regularly speak of the power to soothe, to calm, to tranquillize.

ii. They are used of gentleness of conduct, especially in the case and on the part of people who had it in their power to act far otherwise. They are used of a tyrant wooing the people by the promise of gentle treatment, if he is raised to power. Cyrus the Persian king is described as 'gentle and forgiving of human errors', because he acted kindly towards an officer who had failed in an allotted task. Agesilaus of Sparta was described as cheerful in fear, and gentle in success. Xenophon uses these words for the kindly and patient way in which an officer trained and treated the awkward squad of soldiers. He also uses them for the firm yet sympathetic way in which a horseman trains and disciplines a high-spirited horse. Plato uses these words in the sense of the politeness and the courtesy which are the cement of society. Xenophon uses them of the atmosphere of brotherly understanding which develops between soldiers who have been comrades in arms for long, and who have campaigned together and faced danger and death together. He calls agriculture the gentle art, because in it men learn to co-operate with nature in her forces and in her gifts.

iii. One of the characteristic uses of these words is to describe the right attitude and atmosphere which should prevail in any argument in which questions are being posed and answers demanded and given. So Socrates thanks Thrasymachus that he has left off scolding, and has become gentle. The words are used of taking remarks in good part, and of discussing things without losing one's temper.

It is sometimes easier to see the meaning of a thing by seeing its opposite in operation. Sir Joshua Reynolds said of Dr Johnson: 'The most light and airy dispute was with him a dispute in the arena. He fought on every occasion as if his whole reputation depended upon the victory of the minute, and he fought with all his weapons. If he was foiled in argument, he had recourse to abuse and rudeness.' After a vivid night at the Crown and Anchor Johnson said contentedly to Boswell: 'Well, we had good talk.' To which Boswell dutifully replied: 'Yes, sir, you tossed and gored several persons.' Goldsmith said of Johnson: 'There is no arguing with Johnson; for, when his pistol misses fire, he knocks you down with the butt end of it.' Even the Rev. John Taylor who was a close friend of Johnson said of him: 'There is no disputing with him. He will not hear you, and, having a louder voice than you, must roar you down.' Johnson and *prautēs* were clearly total strangers to each other.

iv. These words are used of taking a thing lightly. Socrates says that he sits lightly to the things which others believe to be valuable. Xenophon uses the words of a man talking lightly of an unpleasant experience, and of the equanimity and the manliness with which Socrates accepted the sentence of death.

v. The words are regularly used of animals which have been tamed, and which have learned to accept discipline and control. A horse obedient to the reins, a dog trained to obey the word of command, is *praus*.

vi. The most characteristic use of these words is to describe the character in which strength and gentleness go together. In Plato the best illustration of *prautēs* is the watchdog who is bravely hostile to strangers and gently friendly with familiars whom he knows and loves. The best and the greatest character, the character of the man who is truly *praus*, is the character which is at once passionate and gentle in the highest degree.

Praus is the word in which strength and gentleness are perfectly combined. The fullest and the best discussion of *prautēs* is in Aristotle, but for the moment we shall leave that and see how the words are used in the Bible itself.

In the LXX there is hardly any sphere of life in which *prautēs* is not of infinite value.

i. *Prautēs* is one of the excellent qualities of a good wife. The Sage says: 'If there be kindness, meekness, and comfort in her tongue, then is her husband not like other men' (Ecclus 36.23). We may remember Shakespeare's line: 'Her voice was ever soft, gentle and low, an excellent thing in women.'

ii. *Prautēs* is the spirit in which a man ought to answer his fellow-men and to go about his business. The Sage urges men to give to the poor man 'a friendly answer with meekness' (Ecclus 4.8). 'My son,' says the Sage, 'go about thy business with meekness; so shalt thou be beloved of him that is approved' (Ecclus 3.17, 18). It is truth, meekness and righteousness which enable a ruler to prosper and to reign (Ps. 45.4). The words come very near to meaning that perfect courtesy to men of every rank and station which is the basis of all right human relationships.

iii. This use of these words leads directly to the third fact about them. Meekness is regularly contrasted with pride. 'The Lord,' says the Sage, 'has cast down the thrones of proud princes and set up the meek in their stead' (Ecclus 10.14). The feet of the meek and lowly shall trample upon the proud (Isa. 26.6). God will vindicate the justice of the meek as opposed to the arrogant hypocrite (Job 36.15). Meekness is the opposite of arrogance and pride.

iv. Sometimes this contrast is even wider. Sometimes the contrast is between the meek man and the sinner. 'The Lord lifts up the meek,' says the Psalmist, 'but brings sinners to the ground' (Ps. 147.6). This meekness is nothing less than the basic quality which keeps a man from sin.

v. Repeatedly in the OT the meek man is the man who is in special favour with God. To such a man God will reveal his secrets. Mysteries are revealed unto the meek (Ecclus 3.19). 'The meek will he guide in judgment, and the meek will he teach his ways' (Ps. 25.9).

vi. Very commonly in the OT the exaltation of the meek is spoken of. The meek shall inherit the earth (Ps. 37.11). God rises up in judgment to save all the meek in heart (Ps. 76.9). The Lord takes pleasure in his people, and will exalt the meek with salvation (Ps. 149.4). The Lord lifts up the meek but brings sinners to the ground (Ps. 147.6). Faith and meekness are his delight (Ecclus 1.27).

vii. So far we have not really been trying to define the meaning of the word; we have been rather trying simply to amass the evidence for such a definition. But before we leave the LXX there is one use of the word which is a main pointer to its meaning. In the OT Moses is the supreme example of meekness. The man Moses was meek, beyond all men that were upon the earth (Num. 12.3). And the Sage repeats this by saying that God sanctified Moses in all his faithfulness and meekness, and chose him out of all men (Ecclus 45.4). The fact that the character of Moses is the great example of meekness lights up this word—and to that we will return.

We now turn to the use of *praus* and *prautēs* in the NT itself. We have a fair amount of material on which to go, for the noun *prautēs* occurs eleven times and the adjective *praus* four times. We shall still confine ourselves to setting out the evidence and we shall not yet try to define the meaning of the words. We shall look first of all at the words with which *praus* keeps company.

i. It keeps company with *agapē*, which is Christian love. Paul asks the Corinthians whether they wish him to come to them with the punishing rod or with meekness and love

(I Cor. 4.21). We have seen that *agapē* means that undefeatable benevolence and that unconquerable goodwill which will never turn to bitterness, and which will always seek a man's highest good, no matter what he does. So, then, there is a connection between love and meekness.

ii. It keeps company with *epieikeia*. *Epieikeia* is surely the most untranslatable word in the NT. Usually it is translated gentleness but it means far more than that. Aristotle spoke of *epieikeia* as the quality which is just and which is sometimes better than justice. He spoke of *epieikeia* as the quality which corrects the law when the law fails because of its generality. There are times when it is necessary to proceed on equity and not on legal justice. There are times when decisions have to be taken, not as the rules and the regulations lay down, but in a spirit which transcends law. There are circumstances which make the strict application of the law unjust, and *epieikeia* is the quality which knows when to forget and to relax the law and to deal with others, not in law, but in mercy and in love. In II Cor. 10.1 Paul puts the two words *prautēs* and *epieikeia* together and uses them both of Jesus, when he speaks of the meekness and the gentleness of Jesus. *Prautēs* is then kin to this great quality which recognizes that there are times when justice can become unjust, and that there are times when there is something higher than the law.

iii. More than once *prautēs* is connected with lowliness and humility. Lowliness and meekness are characteristic of the Christian vocation (Eph. 4.2). The elect of God will clothe themselves with the garment of humility of mind and with meekness (Col. 3.12). Jesus himself is meek and lowly in heart (Matt. 11.29). *Prautēs* has to do with that lowliness and humility in which there is no arrogance and in which there is only the delight to serve.

We must now look at the words with which *prautēs* is contrasted.

i. It is contrasted with stern and condign punishment. We have already quoted the passage in which Paul asks the Corinthians whether they wish him to come to them with the severity of the chastening rod or with meekness and love (I Cor. 4.21). *Prautēs* is the opposite of that stern discipline which inflicts the punishment which strict justice demands.

ii. It is contrasted with the fighting, the belligerent and the pugnacious spirit. In the Pastoral Epistles it is the duty of the Christian minister to urge upon all men that they must not be brawlers, but that they must show all meekness to all men (Titus 3.2). *Prautēs* is the opposite of the aggressive, belligerent spirit which lives at war with men.

We must now look at the part which *prautēs* plays in the Christian life, and here we shall find that *prautēs* is one of the great essentials of the Christian life.

i. *Prautēs* is the spirit in which to learn. Men must receive with meekness the word which is able to save their souls (James 1.21). *Prautēs* is the spirit in which a man knows his own ignorance, in which he is humble enough to know that he does not know, which can open the mind to the truth, and the heart to the love, of God.

ii. *Prautēs* is the spirit in which discipline must be exercised, and in which the faults of others must be corrected. It is Paul's advice that, if a man is overtaken in a fault, he must certainly be corrected, but the correction must be given and applied in the spirit of *prautēs* (Gal. 6.1). Correction can be given in a way which entirely discourages a man and which drives him to depression and to despair; and correction can be given in a way which sets a man upon his feet with the determination to do better and with the hope of doing better. *Prautēs* is the spirit which makes correction a stimulant and not a depressant, a means to hope and not a cause of despair.

iii. *Prautēs* is the spirit in which opposition must be met. In the Pastoral Epistles the Christian minister is urged to instruct those who oppose him with *prautēs* (II Tim. 2.25). Too often we meet those who disagree with us and who differ from us, and whom we think to be mistaken, in a spirit in which we seek to batter and to bludgeon them into changing their minds. Dr Dickie uses an illustration like this. Suppose we go into a room on a bitterly cold day and find that the windows are frozen on the inside, there are two things which we may do. We may try to rub away the ice on the inside of the window panes, but the only result will be that the harder we rub the quicker the ice will reform. Or, we may light a fire in the grate, and the window will clear itself and the ice will melt away. Heat does what friction cannot do. In dealing with those whom we believe to be in error gentleness will do what the bludgeon will never do.

iv. *Prautēs* is the spirit of Christian witness. It is Peter's demand that the Christian must always be ready to give a reason for the hope that is in him—but always with *prautēs* and fear (I Peter 3.15). Real Christian witness has always a gracious gentleness about it which is far more effective than the discourteous kind of witness which tries to ram its opinions down other people's throats. Christian witness must be winsome as well as strong.

v. *Prautēs* is the spirit which ought to pervade the whole of the Christian life. On the whole life and conduct of the man who is wise there will be *prautēs* (James 3.13). The real ornament of life, which is precious in the sight of God and lovely in the sight of men is the meek and quiet spirit (I Peter 3.4). This is the spirit which really commends itself to men and to God.

There remain two things to be said about the NT use of *prautēs*.

i. *Prautēs* is more than something which is gentle and gracious. It is the secret of conquest and of power, for it is the meek who are blessed and who will inherit the earth (Matt. 5.5). *Prautēs* makes a man a king among men.

ii. Finally, we must note that no fewer than three times this quality is connected with Jesus himself. It was Jesus' own invitation : 'Take my yoke upon you and learn of me, for I am meek and lowly in heart' (Matt. 11.29). His triumphal entry into Jerusalem was the fulfilment of the prophecy : 'Behold thy king cometh unto thee, meek and sitting upon an ass' (Zech. 9.9.; Matt. 21.5). It is by the meekness and the gentleness of Christ that Paul appeals to the unruly Corinthians for sympathy and for obedience (II Cor. 10.1). This meekness is of the very essence of the character of Jesus himself.

As we began by saying, nearly all the translations of the NT translate *prautēs* by either meekness or gentleness. The

AV and the RV never vary from meekness. The RSV varies between meekness (II Cor. 10.1; Eph. 4.2; Col. 3.12; James 1.21; 3.13) and gentleness (I Cor. 4.21; Gal. 5.23; 6.1; II Tim. 2.25; I Peter 3.15). Only once does the RSV depart from these translations. In Titus 3.2 it well translates 'showing perfect courtesy to all men'. Moffatt uniformly uses gentleness except in the two James passages. In James 1.21 he has: 'Make a soil of modesty for the word which roots itself inwardly', and in James 3.13 he used the phrase 'the modesty of wisdom'. Weymouth varies widely. He has meekness in Gal. 5.23; 6.1; Col. 3.12; gentleness in II Cor. 10.1; II Tim. 2.25; the tender spirit in I Cor. 4.21; unselfishness in Eph. 4.2; the forgiving spirit in Titus 3.2; the humble spirit in James 1.21; the wisely teachable spirit in James 3.13. Kingsley Williams has gentleness in I Cor. 4.21; Gal. 5.23; 6.1; Eph. 4.2; II Tim. 2.25; Titus 3.2; I Peter 3.15. He has meekness in II Cor. 10.1; Col. 3.12; James 1.21. Only in James 3.13 does he depart from these two renderings, and in that one instance he was 'the humility of wisdom'. The wide variation in the renderings of the translators well shows the difficulty of translating these words.

When we were discussing the meaning of these words in classical Greek, we said that the fullest discussion of them was in Aristotle and to that discussion we now return.

In the little tract *On Virtues and Vices* which is included in Aristotle's works, but which is not his, it is said that *prautēs* and courage both belong to the passionate part of man's nature (1.3); it is then said that *prautēs* is the goodness of the passionate part of a man's nature, and that its possession makes people difficult to move to anger (2.2). Then there comes the fuller definition: 'To *prautēs* belongs the ability to bear reproaches and slights with moderation, and not to embark on revenge quickly, and not to be easily provoked to anger, but to be free from bitterness and contentiousness, having tranquillity and stability in the spirit' (4.3). Now indeed *prautēs* is taking shape and form.

In the *Eudemian Ethics prautēs* is again dealt with. There it is laid down that the opposite of *prautēs* is anger, and that the passionate man is the opposite of the man who is *praus* (2.5.9). Later in the book there comes a fuller and more illuminating definition. To be passionately angry is wrong, and to be slavishly submissive is equally wrong. 'Since, therefore, both these states of character are wrong, it is clear that the state midway between them is right, for it is neither too hasty-tempered nor too slow-tempered, nor does it get angry with the people with whom it ought not, nor fail to get angry with those with whom it ought' (3.3.4). The man who is *praus* is midway between the slavish man and the harsh man.

But the fullest treatment of *prautēs* is in the *Nicomachean Ethics*. For Aristotle every virtue is the mean between two extremes. On the one hand there is the extreme of excess and on the other hand there is the extreme of defect and between them there is the happy medium. Aristotle says that *prautēs* is the mean between *orgilotēs*, which is excessive anger, and *aorgēsia*, which is excessive angerlessness. *Prautēs* is the mean between too much and too little anger; the man who is *praus* is the man with just the right amount of anger in his make-up (2.7.10). *Prautēs*, he goes on to say is the observance of the mean in relation to anger. The man who is *praus* is the man who feels anger 'on the right grounds, and against the right persons, and in the right manner, and at the right moment, and for the right length of time.' But at all times he will err on the side of forgiveness rather than on the side of anger (4.5.1-4). Here then is the meaning of *praus*. The man who is *praus* is the man who is always angry at the right time and never angry at the wrong time.

And here is the reason why Moses is the great example of *prautēs*. Moses was no spineless creature. The phase 'as meek as Moses' is quite wrongly used. Moses was a man who could be blazingly angry when anger was needed and who could yet be humbly submissive when submission was needed. No spineless, spiritless, anaemic creature could have lead men as Moses did. Moses had strength and gentleness combined. And what was true of Moses was truer still of Jesus Christ, for in Jesus there was righteous anger and there was forgiving love. Only a man who was *praus* could have both cleansed the Temple of the hucksters who traded in it and forgiven the woman taken in adultery whom all the orthodox condemned.

The root meaning of *prautēs* is self-control. It is the complete control of the passionate part of our nature. It is when we have *prautēs* that we treat all men with perfect courtesy, that we can rebuke without rancour, that we can argue without intolerance, that we can face the truth without resentment, that we can be angry and yet sin not, that we can be gentle and yet not weak. *Prautēs* is the virtue in which our relationships both with ourselves and our fellow-men become perfect and complete.

Clearly no man can win that self-control for himself and by himself. The passions break their leash and are too strong for the will and the reason which would hold them in check. And that is precisely why *prautēs* is part of the fruit of the Spirit; for such self-control can only come when we are God-controlled through the help of the Spirit of God. *Prautēs* is the power through which by the help of the Spirit of God the strong and explosive might of the passions is harnessed in the service of men and of God.

EGKRATEIA

The Victory over Desire

The ninth and last grace in the fruit of the Spirit is *egkrateia*, which the AV translates temperance; the RV retains this translation, but in the margin gives self-control, which is by far the better translation.

In the NT itself we have very little material through which to work out the meaning of this word. In the NT it occurs in only two other places. Paul reasoned with the Roman governor Felix and his wife Drusilla about righteousness and temperance (Acts 24.25). The writer of II Peter bids his readers to add temperance to knowledge, and patience to temperance (II Peter 1.6).

The corresponding verb *egkrateuomai* occurs twice in the NT. It means to be self-controlled or to exercise self-control.

In I Cor. 7.9 Paul, speaking of the relationship between the sexes, advises against marriage, but then adds: 'If they cannot contain, let them marry.' That is to say, if self-control proves impossible, then marriage is permissible. In I Cor. 9.25 he lays down the universal principle that every man who strives for the mastery is temperate in all things.

The corresponding adjective *egkratēs* occurs once in the NT. It means self-controlled. In Titus 1.8 it is laid down of the elders that they must be sober, just, holy, and temperate.

Clearly the NT itself provides very little material for the elucidation of the meaning of this word.

The LXX does not use these words frequently either, but the few instances of them in the LXX do help to give content to their meaning. Ecclus 18.30 begins a section entitled Temperance of the Soul. That phrase is the heading of the section. The section reads: 'Go not after thy lusts, but refrain thyself from thine appetites. If thou givest thy soul the desires that please her, she will make thee a laughing-stock to thine enemies that malign thee. Take not pleasure in much good cheer, neither be tied to the expense thereof. Be not made a beggar by banqueting upon borrowing, when thou hast nothing in thy purse, for thou shalt lie in wait for thine own life, and be talked about' (Ecclus 18.30-33). From this passage it is clear that *egkrateia* at least includes self-restraint and self-control and self-discipline in matters of bodily and physical pleasure.

The word occurs again in 4 Maccabees. That book tells of the terrible persecution of the Jews under Antiochus Epiphanes, who made a deliberate and savage attempt to wipe out Jewish religion. Eleazar is brought before the persecutors and is given the choice between eating swine's flesh and death. His answer is: 'I will not fail thee, O Law, my instructor! I will not foresake thee, O beloved Temperance!' (4 Macc. 5.4). There the word describes the self-restraint, the self-discipline, the self-denial which will not break the Jewish food laws, even if it is death to keep them.

The verb *egkrateuesthai* occurs in the LXX in the sense of restraining oneself from doing something, or, as the AV has it in archaic English, refraining oneself from doing something. When Joseph recognized his brothers, and in particular when he recognized Benjamin, he was overcome by his emotion. He retired to hide his emotion and his tears. Then he washed his face and went out and in their presence refrained himself (Gen. 43.31). That is to say, he restrained his emotion. Similarly in Esther Haman is enraged at the prosperity of Mordecai, but for the moment he refrained himself (Esth. 5.10). That is, for the moment he restrained his anger.

In the LXX *egkratēs* is quite common, but not in the ethical sense. All these words have as their root the verb *kratein* which means to take hold of, to grip. Thus *egkratēs* can simply mean to be in possession of, or to take hold of (Tob. 6.3; Ecclus 6.27; 15.1; 27.30; II Macc. 8.30; 10.15, 17; 13.13). This is in fact a valuable sidelight on the ethical meaning of the word; for when the word enters the moral and the ethical sphere it describes that strength of soul by which a man takes a hold of himself, takes a grip of himself, is in full control and possession of himself, so that he can restrain himself from every evil desire. In the LXX it seems to occur only once in the ethical sense. The Sage declares that 'a shamefaced and faithful woman is a double grace, and her *continent* mind is beyond value' (Ecclus 26.15). There the word describes the strong chastity which has every passion under complete control.

In classical Greek the word emerges in Plato as a moral and an ethical word. Plato speaks of *egkrateia*, mastery of pleasures and desires (*Republic* 430 E). In the *Memorabilia* Xenophon records of Socrates that he was of all men the most master of the desires of love and appetite (*Memorabilia* 1.2.1). As in the case of *prautēs*, the word *egkrateia* is very fully discussed by Aristotle, but we shall leave the examination of his treatment of the word till the end.

Since then, when we go to times earlier than the NT, we do not find much material to help in the definition of *egkrateia*, we may in this case try to discover what help we can find by going forward. The first group of Christian writers outside the NT wrote in the very late years of the first century and in the first half of the second century, and they are known as the Apostolic Fathers. They are obviously of first-rate importance for the study of the thought of the early Church, and they have a great deal to say about *egkrateia*, and of its place in the Christian life.

i. It is a gift of God, and one of the greatest gifts of God. 'How blessed and wonderful are the gifts of God!' writes Clement of Rome, and then he goes on to enumerate some of them : 'Life in immortality, splendour in righteousness, truth in boldness, faith in confidence, continence (*egkrateia*) in holiness' (*I Clement* 35.1, 2). Temperance (*egkrateia*), says Hermas, is like every gift of God. It is twofold, for there are some things from which it is a duty to refrain, and there are some things from which it is a duty not to refrain (*The Shepherd of Hermas, Mandates* 8.1). Clement has a noble passage on the excellencies of the Christian life : 'Let the strong care for the weak, and let the weak reverence the strong. Let the rich man bestow help on the poor, and let the poor give thanks to God that God gave him someone to supply his needs. Let the wise manifest his wisdom, not in words but in good deeds. Let him who is humble-minded not testify to his own humility, but let him leave it to others to bear him witness. Let him who is pure in the flesh not be boastful, knowing that it is another who bestows on him his continence' (*I Clement* 38.2). The very last prayer of Clement for those to whom he writes is : 'Now may God, the all-seeing and the master of spirits, and the Lord of all flesh, who chose out the Lord Jesus Christ, and us through him for a peculiar people, give unto every soul that is called after his glorious and holy name, faith, fear, peace, patience and long-suffering, self-control, purity, sobriety, that they may be well-pleasing to his name (*I Clement* 64). In a tainting world the early teachers loved *egkrateia* and saw it as one of the greatest gifts of God.

ii. It is part of the very basis of the Christian life. Clement in bringing his letter to a close writes : 'We have touched on every aspect of faith and repentance and true love and self-control and sobriety and patience' (*I Clement* 62.2). *Egkrateia* is one of the foundation pillars on which the Christian life is supported. According to Hermas, *egkrateia* is part of the first commandment of the Christian life.

The angel says to him : 'I command you in the first commandment to keep faith and fear and continence' (*The Shepherd of Hermas, Mandates* 6.1).

iii. It is the ally of the Christian life. The letter of Barnabas has it : 'Fear and patience are the helpers of our faith, long-suffering and continence are its allies' (*The Letter of Barnabas* 2.2).

iv. It is the way to save the soul. The angel says to Hermas : 'You are saved by not having broken away from the living God and by your simplicity and great temperance' (*The Shepherd of Hermas, Visions* 2.3.2). In *II Clement* it is said : 'Now I think that I have given no mean advice concerning self control, and, if any man follow it, he shall have no regret, but shall save both himself and me his counsellor' (*II Clement* 15.1).

v. It is the mark of Christian love. Polycarp sets down the lesson that Christian wives must learn : 'Next teach our wives to remain in the faith given to them, and in love and purity, tenderly loving their husbands in all truth, and loving others equally in all *chastity*, and to educate their children in the fear of God' (Polycarp, *Philippians* 4.2). It is *egkrateia* which makes love chastity and not lust.

vi. It is the support of the Christian Church. In his *Visions* Hermas sees a tower being built, and the tower is the symbol of the Church. Round the tower there were seven women and the tower was supported by them. 'The second who is girded and looks like a man is called Continence; and she is the daughter of faith. Whosoever then shall follow her becomes blessed in his life, because he will abstain from all evil deeds, believing that, if he refrains from every evil lust, he will inherit eternal life' (*The Shepherd of Hermas, Visions* 3.8.4). One of the supports and buttresses of the Christian Church and the Christian life is *egkrateia*.

The value that the early teachers set on the virtue of *egkrateia* is clear. And the self-restraint, the self-control, the self-discipline, the purity and the chastity in the word are clear.

It is Aristotle who has the great classical discussion of the word. He, or his disciple, deals with it in the little tractate *On Virtues and Vices*. It is there said that *egkrateia* is the virtue of the appetitive part of the soul (1.3). It is later more fully defined: 'To *egkrateia* belongs the ability to restrain desire by reason, when it is set on base enjoyments and pleasures, and to be resolute and ever in readiness to endure natural want and pain' (5.1).

In the *Eudemian Ethics egkrateia* is again dealt with. There Aristotle deals with the man who is the opposite of *egkratēs*, the man who is *akratēs*. He writes: 'All wickedness makes a man more unrighteous, and lack of self-control seems to be wickedness; the uncontrolled man is the sort of man to act in conformity to desire contrary to calculation; and he shows his lack of control, when his conduct is guided by desire; so that the uncontrolled man will act unrighteously by acting in conformity with desire' (2.7.6). The opposite of *egkrateia* is action dominated by desire, and the man who is *egkratēs* is the man who prevents desire from being the dictator of his actions and his life.

The fullest discussion of *egkrateia* is in the seventh book of the *Nicomachean Ethics* and it is of the greatest interest and importance. Aristotle begins by defining the man who is *egkratēs* by his opposite, the man who is *akratēs*. The man who is *egkratēs* is self-restrained, the man who is *akratēs* is unrestrained (7.1.1). These two words in fact give us the clue and the key to the whole matter. Both are connected with the verb *kratein*, which means to grip, to grasp, to hold, to control. The man who is *egkratēs* has a controlling grip and hold of himself, the man who is *akratēs* has no grip or hold of himself. Then Aristotle goes on to speak of the things with which *akrasia*, the quality of the man who is *akratēs*, is connected. It is connected with *malakia*, which is softness in living, and with *truphē*, which is sensuous and sensual luxury in living (7.1.4). On the other hand it is contrasted with *karteria*, which is steadfast fortitude and endurance.

Aristotle then goes on to lay down the essential differences between certain types of character. The man who is *sōphrōn*, prudent and temperate, is always self-restrained and enduring. The man who is *akratēs* does things which are wrong, but he does not do them by choice; he does them when he is swept away by impulse and by passion, and he knows that he is doing wrong in a sense against his will and judgment. Desire has forced him to depart from the course of action which reason tells him is good. The man who is *akolastos* does things which are wrong quite deliberately; he is the profligate who quite deliberately chooses the way of desire. The man who is *egkratēs* has strong desires which seek to lure and force him from the way of reason, but he has them under control (7.1.6, 7; 7.2.6, 7).

But wherein is this area of desire and of unrestraint? In this life there are two kinds of pleasure—necessary and unnecessary. The necessary pleasures are the pleasures of the natural instincts; the unnecessary pleasures are money, gain, honour and such things. Now you can say that a man is unrestrained in his desire for money or for fame, but in such a case you do not say that he is *unrestrained*, as it were, *simpliciter*; you state the area in which he is unrestrained. When you use the word *unrestrained* without qualification of any man, what is meant is that he is unrestrained in regard to bodily pleasures and pains (7.4.1-4).

Here we have the essence of the whole matter. *Egkrateia* is nothing other than chastity, and chastity was the one completely new virtue which the Christian ethic brought into this world. *Egkrateia* is that great quality which comes to a man when Christ is in his heart, that quality which makes him able to live and to walk in the world, and yet to keep his garments unspotted from the world.